Leckie×Leckie
Scotland's leading educational publishers

Success guides

HIGHER
Psychology

D0178806

× JONATHAN FIRTH ×

Contents

Conformity and Obedience

Social Relationships

Atypical Behaviour

Intelligence

Icons and features

Make the Link

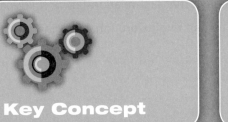

Key Concept

Top Tips

The nature of attachment

What is attachment?

When infants are looked after by adults they form a long-term **emotional bond** known as an **attachment**, connecting them together in a relationship.

Separation causes stress and sadness. The key **behavioural** feature of attachment is trying to maintain close **proximity** (Ainsworth and Bell, 1970).

The strongest attachment a child has is called the **primary attachment**, and the person whom the child bonds with in this way is their **primary attachment figure** (or **PAF**).

Key features of attachment

Wanting close proximity to the caregiver, as separation brings distress.	
Using the attachment figure as a secure base to explore the world.	
Orienting behaviour towards the attachment figure, e.g. looking at them, facing towards them.	

(Maccoby, 1980)

The importance of attachment

Forming a secure attachment is important for a child's wellbeing. Later in this topic there are examples of what happens when this goes wrong, or if a child does not have an opportunity to develop an attachment bond.

It is clear that attachment to others plays a role in **early socialisation**, i.e. how a child learns to become part of human society. Bowlby (1969) believed that the relationship with the PAF provides a **prototype** for future **relationships**. In other words, through that first relationship, a child learns how to deal with people in later life.

Attachment has played a role in human **evolution** – maintaining proximity and forming bonds with caregivers helped our ancestors to survive.

Research into attachment

In an observational study of attachment, Schaffer and Emerson (1964) observed 60 infants in their homes in Glasgow once every four weeks for a year, and then again at age 18 months. Attachment was measured by asking the mothers about **separation protest** – how their child responded to being separated in everyday situations such as being left outside in a pram. The researchers also measured **stranger anxiety** by approaching the infants at the start of every visit and noting when they started to whimper.

The infants showed their first **specific attachment** at 6–8 months, and stranger anxiety appeared around a month later. Soon after, multiple attachments started to form.

In 39% of cases, the child's PAF was **not** the person who fed and bathed them, and there was little connection between the strength of an attachment and how much time the child spent with that person. Instead, mothers who interacted with their babies **responsively** tended to have the strongest bond.

A weakness of the study is its reliance on the mothers' reports of separation protest, which may have been unreliable.

Graph adapted from Schaffer and Emerson (1964)

Stages of attachment

The main changes in attachment through infancy can be displayed as stages, although the ages at which these occur will vary.

Name of stage	Age	Key features
Pre-attachment	0–2 months	Enjoys social contact, indiscriminate liking of any carer
Attachment-in-the-making	2–7 months	Recognises familiar people, but still content with strangers
Specific attachment	7 months plus	Separation protest when PAF leaves; stranger anxiety
Multiple attachments	9 months plus	Attachments to other familiar people, but PAF is still preferred

(Based on Schaffer, 1996)

Multiple attachments occur from the age of around nine months onwards. This is when a child begins to show strong bonds with one or more carers in addition to the PAF. This could be the other parent, a sibling or grandparent, for example.

As the child develops new relationships, the bond to the PAF tends to remain strongest. However, Lamb (1981) states that rather than being attached to different degrees, children form **different types of attachments** to their father and mother.

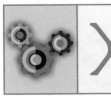

| Attachment | Stranger anxiety | PAF – primary attachment figure |
| Prototype | Stages of attachment | Separation protest |

Quick Test 1

1. What are the key features of attachment?

Historical views of attachment

The behaviourist approach

Behaviourist psychology tried to show that human behaviour was the product of learning. Research from this perspective tended to use animals in laboratories. For example, Ivan Pavlov (1927) found that dogs learned to **associate** the presence of food with the ringing of a bell. This process of learning by association became known as **classical conditioning**. Behaviourists thought that **attachment** worked in the same way – the infant learns to associate the mother with food, and therefore becomes attached to her.

Operant conditioning means learning the outcome of our actions. When an action leads to some kind of reward, the behaviour becomes stronger or more frequent. Something which strengthens behaviour in this way is called a **reinforcer**. Dollard and Miller (1950) believed that food is a **primary reinforcer**, something that is directly rewarding from birth – this does not need to be learned. A carer who provides the food is a **secondary reinforcer**. Initially they are not a source of reward but, when an infant learns to **associate them** with food, their presence becomes rewarding in its own right.

Research into behaviourist approach	Evaluation
Harlow (1959) conducted a study in which infant monkeys were taken away from their mothers and placed in a cage containing a wire mother-like figure with a feeding bottle, and a soft, cloth mother-like figure which did not have a feeding bottle. If attachments are formed through association with feeding, then the infant monkeys should have become attached to the wire 'mother'. In fact, they only used the wire mother to feed, and preferred clinging to the cloth figure, particularly when frightened. The pleasure infants get from being held or cuddled is called **contact comfort**.	The concept of primary and secondary reinforcers has been demonstrated in laboratory experiments, and can explain why babies and small children like to be close to their parents and carers. However, Harlow's research suggests that, rather than learning attachment through classical conditioning, we have an innate drive for contact comfort.

Harlow's monkey clinging to cloth mother-like figure.

Top Tip

Referring to research evidence can pick up analysis and evaluation (A & E) marks in an exam answer.

Top Tip

If it is not specified in the question, correctly stating a researcher's name and year can gain a mark.

The psychoanalytic approach

Freud's **psychoanalytic approach** sets out a series of stages through which a child develops and, in each stage, a different part of the body is the focus for pleasure. The earliest stage is the **oral stage**, where an infant gets pleasure through the mouth – from feeding. Freud believed that at an early stage of childhood the rational **ego** has not yet developed. Instead, the child is entirely ruled by the unconscious mind or **id**, which is focused on seeking pleasure – this is known as the **pleasure principle**. A child will therefore demand to be fed.

Research into psychoanalytic approach	Evaluation
Melanie Klein was one of the first psychoanalysts to do research with children. She observed that very young babies show aggression when the mother doesn't meet their needs (Klein, 1957). From around four months of age, they begin to show guilt for this aggression. Klein called this the 'depressive position', and believed it to be the start of forming a healthy, loving bond with the mother.	The concept of the pleasure principle helps to explain why infants become attached to their carer. However, the theory is based on vague and speculative ideas. It is difficult to prove or disprove this theory – it can't be **falsified**. This makes it unscientific.

Top Tip

In the Higher exam, any suitable research studies will be credited – they don't need to be the ones you have studied in class.

For more information on the behaviourist and psychoanalytic approaches, see the chapter on 'Atypical Behaviour' on page 82.

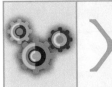

Conditioning   Primary and secondary reinforcer   Contact comfort

Oral stage   Pleasure principle

Quick Test 2

1. Which type of conditioning is based on reward and punishment?
2. What is the oral stage?

The Bowlby–Ainsworth paradigm

Bowlby's attachment theory

Contemporary attachment theory draws on the work of John Bowlby, who was commissioned by the World Health Organisation to write a report on the mental health of homeless children (Bowlby, 1951). He famously said that:

> 'mother love in infancy is as important to mental health as are vitamins and proteins for physical health.'

Key features of Bowlby's attachment theory

Attachment figure as a base	One key attachment
An attachment figure is a secure base from which the infant can explore the environment. Infants cling to adults who can protect them against danger (Bowlby, 1969).	Infants tend to form a close relationship with one person. Bowlby called this phenomenon **monotropy**, meaning a tendency to focus on one person. Separation from this individual causes distress.
Critical period for attachment	**Social releasers**
Bowlby at first asserted that there was a **critical period of infant development** during which secure attachment **must** be formed, though this was later modified to a 'sensitive period', i.e. the best time to form an attachment.	**Social releasers** are behaviours which stimulate bonding with the parents, such as when a child smiles, reaches out or cries. Social releasers have evolved to help the child get its parents' attention, improving survival chances.

Ainsworth's theories

In her observations of families, Mary Ainsworth believed she had identified that differences in the way mothers responded to their infants led to those infants being more or less **secure** in their attachment. She also felt that the more insecure children fell into two categories – insecure (avoidant), who **avoided comforting**, and insecure (resistant) who were overly **clingy**.

The strange situation

This laboratory experiment by Ainsworth and Bell (1970) involved a baby with its mother (or other attachment figure) and a stranger. There are several phases, most of which last for three minutes:

- The mother and baby are introduced to a room with toys, and are left to play and explore.
- A stranger enters and speaks to the mother, then approaches the infant with a toy.
- The mother leaves the child alone with the stranger, and the stranger tries to interact with the child, and then the mother returns. This happens twice.

The findings of the study confirmed that there are three main **attachment types**. The behaviours of these types were as follows:

Type A – Insecure (avoidant) infants focused on toys when their mother was present, were not fearful of strangers, and avoided contact on the mother's return.

Type B – Securely attached infants explored happily when their mother was present, were fearful of strangers, and enthusiastic on the mother's return. This was the most common type.

Type C – Insecure (resistant) infants were unwilling to explore. They were highly fearful of strangers, and showed anger on the mother's return.

Evaluation

- Has become a widely used technique for studying attachment
- Unclear whether it shows the characteristics of the child or of their relationship with one particular adult

Top Tip

Candidates tend to waste time writing lengthy descriptions of the procedure of this experiment. Practise summarising it in under 100 words. Using bullet points is acceptable here.

Cultural differences

Subsequent studies have shown that the frequency of the main attachment types appears to vary by country. In a review of studies, Van Ijzendoorn and Kroonenberg (1988) found the highest proportion of type B (securely attached) infants in Britain and Sweden. European countries tended to have higher levels of type A than type C, while in Israel and Japan, the opposite was true.

According to Ainsworth's theory, this could relate to **cultural differences** in parenting style and responsiveness in different countries. A limitation is that in some countries only one or two studies have been done, so it is hard to draw firm conclusions.

Country	No. of studies	Percentage of each attachment type		
		Type B (Securely attached)	Type A (Insecure-avoidant)	Type C (Insecure-resistant)
West Germany	3	57	35	8
Great Britain	1	75	22	3
Netherlands	4	67	26	7
Sweden	1	74	22	4
Israel	2	64	7	29
Japan	2	68	5	27
China	1	50	25	25
US	18	65	21	14

Table showing percentage of children displaying attachment types in eight countries (Van Ijzendoorn and Kroonenberg, 1988).

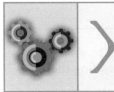

Sensitive period	Monotropy	Social releasers
Secure attachment	Avoidant	Resistant

Quick Test 3

1. Which was the most common of Ainsworth's three attachment types?

Separation and maternal deprivation

Bowlby and maternal deprivation

Bowlby's **maternal deprivation hypothesis** (MDH) states that children are harmed if they are deprived of their mothers at a young age. It is based on his ideas of **monotropy** and the **critical period**: the mother is unique, and attachments must form during the first two to three years.

The study of John

Robertson and Robertson (1969) conducted a study into the effects of short separations. They **observed** a 17-month-old boy named **John**, whose parents had chosen to put him into residential care for nine days while his mother was in hospital having another baby. John tried unsuccessfully to get a nurse to 'mother' him, and protested aggressively when his father left after short visits.

From the third day John became very distressed and cried sadly for long periods. By the seventh day he was in despair. He would not eat and didn't even play. He did not respond to attempts to cheer him up, and lay silently on the floor. When he was reunited with his mother, he was angry and did not want to sit with her.

Top Tip

This is a study of a short-term separation.

Analysis of John's behaviour

John's separation caused **distress**, which has three components:

- Protest – angry outbursts, clinging to the parent when they leave.
- Despair – calmer behaviour but inwardly upset; responds less to others.
- Detachment – begins to respond to others again but in a superficial way. If reunited, may reject the parent and have to 'relearn' a relationship.

The researchers believed that John's problems were due to **bond disruption**, and could have been reduced by providing a **substitute** carer while his mother was away.

Evaluation of the study of John

This study was highly influential, encouraging hospitals to relax their strict visiting hours. In a follow-up study, a girl was provided with substitute emotional care and became considerably less distressed, supporting the researchers' conclusions.

The 44 thieves

Bowlby noticed from his clinical work that some children who committed crimes and misdemeanours showed no guilt for their actions, and he believed that, due to **maternal deprivation**, they had failed to develop concern for others. Bowlby called this condition **affectionless psychopathy**.

Bowlby (1944) conducted a study on 44 'thieves' – children from his child guidance clinic who had been in trouble for stealing. A further 44 children were used as a control group – they also had emotional problems, but had not committed crimes. Bowlby conducted interviews with the children and their parents.

Fourteen thieves showed affectionless psychopathy, compared to just three of the control group. Out of the fourteen, 86% had been away from their mothers during their early years for six months or more. None of the control group had experienced maternal deprivation.

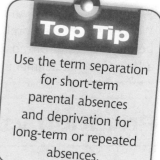

Top Tip

Use the term separation for short-term parental absences and deprivation for long-term or repeated absences.

Evaluation

The **44 thieves study** appears to provide strong support for the MDH. Bowlby's findings suggest that in the **long-term**, maternal deprivation harms emotional development and makes children more likely to get into trouble.

However, all of the data was retrospective – it relied on recall of events which happened years earlier, and may have been unreliable. The diagnosis of affectionless psychopathy was made by Bowlby himself, and so may have been subject to bias.

In a large-scale study of families in the Isle of Wight, Rutter (1976) concluded that **discord** in the family home was more damaging than deprivation.

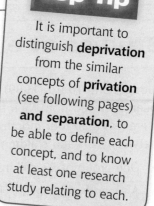

Top Tip

It is important to distinguish **deprivation** from the similar concepts of **privation** (see following pages) **and separation**, to be able to define each concept, and to know at least one research study relating to each.

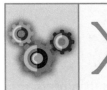

Maternal deprivation	Separation	Distress
Bond disruption	Affectionless psychopathy	

Quick Test 4

1. What are the three stages of distress?
2. Which two of Bowlby's ideas was the MDH based on?

Privation

What is the effect on an infant of growing up without a caregiver, for example in an orphanage? Spitz and Wolf (1946) studied orphanage infants in the USA and Canada and found that a third of the children died before their third birthday, despite receiving good nutrition and healthcare. Researchers began to realise that a lack of any attachment is severely **harmful**.

Privation vs deprivation

Rutter (1981) drew a distinction between a total lack of an attachment figure, and cases where an attachment forms but is later disrupted or lost:

> • PRIVATION: the **lack** of an attachment bond
>
> • DEPRIVATION: the **loss** of an attachment bond

Studies of ex-institutionalised children

Hodges and Tizard (1989) conducted a longitudinal study of children who had been removed from their families and placed in **institutional care** when they were less than four months old. The care home **discouraged attachments** between staff and children. After age two, one of two things happened to them:

Top Tip

Harlow's (1959) study of rhesus monkeys is also an example of privation.

• One group of 23 children were **adopted.**

• A second group of 11 children were **restored** to their natural parents.

The researchers used interviews with the participants and their mothers and a questionnaire for their school teachers. A **control group** was used for comparison.

Findings

• **Adopted** children showed a stronger bond with family members compared to **restored** children.

• All ex-institutionalised children were more **attention-seeking** and had fewer close **friendships** than peers.

Conclusion: Recovery from institutionalisation is possible, but privation does have a lasting effect. A **good family environment** is highly beneficial.

Evaluation: This longitudinal research provided detailed data, but the sample size was very small.

> Rutter *et al.* (1998) studied 111 Romanian orphans who were adopted in the UK aged two or younger after severe privation in their home country. By age four, their IQ and language scores were only slightly lower than normal.
>
> It was concluded that with the right care, early privation can be overcome. A criticism of the study is that functioning at age two was based only on what adoptive parents could remember.

Case-studies

Koluchová (1991) reports the case of twins who were treated cruelly and badly **neglected** by their stepmother up until age seven, after which they were taken into care and later placed in a foster family. The twins recovered remarkably well, going on to attend mainstream school. However, this case is unusual because, as twins, the boys had each other, even if they did not have an adult attachment figure.

Curtiss (1977) describes the case of Genie, a girl who was raised in almost total isolation by her parents. When discovered at age 13, she couldn't speak more than a few words, was very fearful, and seemed much younger than her real age. Sadly, Genie did not recover anything approaching normal language and interaction, perhaps because she was discovered so late in her childhood.

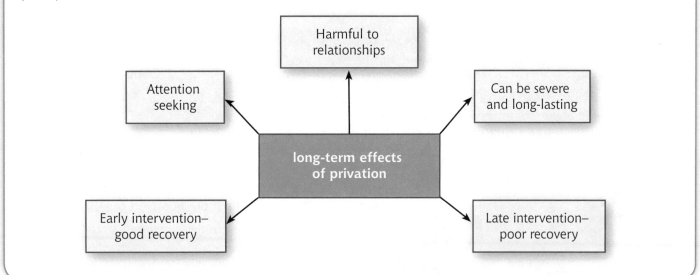

Summary

The variation between individual cases makes it hard to draw conclusions in this area. Overall, it is clear that privation is extremely harmful to a child. With the right care, children do seem to be able to recover and form relationships later in life, though some damage from their early experiences tends to be evident. The earlier (younger) they are put into a good quality, loving, foster/adoptive home, the better the recovery tends to be.

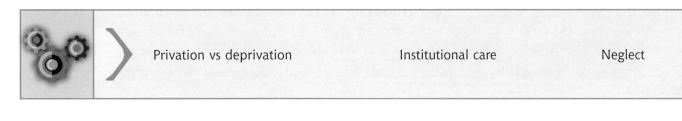

Privation vs deprivation   Institutional care   Neglect

Quick Test 5

1. Which process is characterised by the lack of an attachment bond forming?
2. Name the researcher and year of a case-study into privation.

Day care

Day care means the care of children outside the home and by people other than family, primarily by **nurseries** and **childminders**.

Effects of day care

Bowlby (1953) believed separations from the PAF to be harmful, stating that

> 'leaving any child of under three years of age is ... only to be undertaken for good and sufficient reasons.'

Supporting Bowlby's view, Belsky and Rovine (1987) found that children placed in day care aged eight months or under were more likely to display an 'insecure' attachment on a **strange situation test**. Baydar and Brooks-Gunn (1991) studied

1100 children, and compared those whose mothers went out to work before age one to those whose mothers started work later. The former were more prone to aggressiveness and hyperactivity, and did more poorly in cognitive tests.

However, there are some positive findings. Clarke-Stewart (1989) found that 150 two-to-four-year-olds who attended nursery had better **cognitive development**. Durkin (1995) found that, although day care staff behave differently from mothers, children relate happily to them. Familiar caregivers are not forgotten, and the mother remains the preferred attachment figure when a child is upset.

Research into day care quality

Schaffer (1996) found that as long as day care is good **quality** and stable (not frequently changed), it is fairly harmless and can even be beneficial. Poor quality day care can put a child's **development** at risk with poorer scores on cognitive and social tests. High quality day care seems to be of greater benefit to children from low-income families, who do better at school and socially in later life (Scarr, 1998).

Aspects affecting **day care quality** include the **variety** of activities/play equipment and the **staff to child ratio**.

Summary

Overall there seem to be three major aspects which influence the effects of day care on children:

- The quality of the day care setting
- The family/social background of the child
- How early and for how long the child is left

Good quality childcare can benefit a child's **development**. Studies of children **under the age of one** suggest that caution is needed for separations at this age, as **emotional development** can be put at risk.

Evaluation of research

Scarr (1998) points out that children from **low-income** families are more likely to experience poor quality day care. In studies of day care quality, the effects of these two variables (social background and quality) are therefore hard to separate.

There is a risk of **cultural bias**, as most of the contemporary research took place in the USA, and child-rearing styles can vary widely between cultures.

Top Tip

The A & E demand of a question should be clear from the wording. Any question starting with 'evaluate', 'discuss' or 'explain' will expect some analytical points or evaluation.

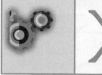

Consider how this subtopic relates to Modern Studies, Sociology and Economics.

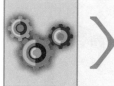

Nursery	Childminder	Development
Quality of day care	Social background	Cultural bias

Sample exam questions

1. Describe and evaluate Bowlby's theories of attachment, referring to research evidence. (8, 4)
2. Discuss the effects of day care on a child. Refer to research evidence in your answer. (8, 4)
3. Describe and briefly evaluate the Psychoanalytic and Behaviourist theories of attachment. (8, 4)
4. Explain the stages of attachment in human infants, with reference to research evidence. (8, 4)

Quick Test 6

1. What aspects of a child's development might day care impact on?
2. Name two things which affect the quality of day care.

The nature of memory

The limits of STM

Human short-term memory (STM) is very limited. Miller (1956) studied its **capacity** and found that no matter what type of item is stored, STM could only hold between five and nine items. This became known as the 'magic number, seven plus or minus two', although more recent researchers have described its capacity as the number of items which can be pronounced in just under two seconds (Schweickert and Boruff, 1986).

The **duration** of STM is also limited to around 30 seconds unless information is **rehearsed** (Peterson and Peterson, 1959).

STM uses **acoustic encoding**, i.e. information represented in STM as sounds.

Type of encoding

Baddeley (1966) aimed to find out the types of **encoding** used by STM and LTM (long-term memory). Different lists of items were used, some of which were acoustically similar (sounded alike) such as 'can, cad, cab, cap', and some of which were semantically similar (similar in meaning), such as 'large, big, huge, broad'.

Over the short term, retrieval of **acoustically similar** lists was poorest. This showed that similar sounding items were mixed up in STM. After a 20-minute delay, poorest recall was with **semantically similar** lists. This showed that items of similar meaning get mixed up in LTM. Baddeley concluded that STM uses acoustic encoding and LTM uses semantic encoding.

Baddeley (1966) used lists of words.

This was a well-controlled study, but doesn't explain what happens to visual information. Also, lists of words are only one of the many things that humans have to remember.

The nature of LTM

LTM is the permanent memory store: information can be encoded to LTM straight away, and can last a lifetime. There is no limit to how much can be stored (unlike a computer hard drive, the LTM doesn't seem to get full).

As explained above, LTM tends to encode information semantically, i.e. based on the **meaning** of an item – if you think of a recent conversation, you can probably remember the gist of what people said, but not their exact words! This form of LTM allows us to store **information**, and is called **semantic memory**.

There are two other LTM stores: **episodic** and **procedural**. Episodic memory is your 'mental diary', remembering things that happened to you. Procedural is your memory for skills such as playing a musical instrument or riding a bike.

Type of LTM	Definition	Example
Episodic	Memory for events	What you did yesterday
Semantic	Memory for information	Remembering a story
Procedural	Memory for skills	How to cycle

The memory process

In both STM and LTM, information goes through a three-stage **process**: it is **encoded** into a memory trace, **stored**, and then **retrieved** when needed.

Encoding involves taking information from the senses or from another memory store and placing it into a memory code. As explained above, STM uses **acoustic** encoding and LTM uses **semantic** encoding. If items are encoded visually, this would be called **visual** encoding.

Storage involves retaining information to be used at a later date. Memories must be **consolidated** in order to be retained, for example, in revising for exams. Walker *et al.* (2003) found that unbroken sleep is vital to the brain processes involved in procedural memories being consolidated.

Retrieval is where information is brought back from the memory store when needed. Sometimes retrieval is difficult: things may be on the **tip of your tongue!** There are two types of retrieval: **free recall** and **recognition**. A cue is a hint or trigger which helps retrieval, such as the letter a word starts with.

Top Tip

Full marks are generally **not** given for exam answers with no named research cited.

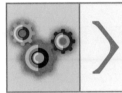

STM – short-term memory	LTM – long-term memory	Encoding
Storage	Retrieval	Free recall
Recognition	Acoustic	Semantic

Quick Test 7

1. What is the capacity of STM?
2. What are the three stages of the memory process?

The multi-store model

The **multi-store model** or **MSM** is a useful but simplistic model of memory devised by Atkinson and Shiffrin (1968). It features the two main 'stores' of memory – short-term memory (STM) and long-term memory (LTM) – and a third store: **sensory memory** (SM).

Top Tip

Note that several key elements in memory come in 3s – three processes, three stores, three types of LTM. Can you find any more?

Sensory memory

Sensory memory comprises a set of stores, one for each sense – sight, hearing, touch, etc. A lot of sensory information enters SM, but only information which a person **pays attention to** is **transferred to STM**, and everything else fades away.

An example of SM in action is when a person speaks to you when you are not paying attention. If you switch attention within a couple of seconds, you still retain a sensory trace of what was said (allowing you to pretend you were listening!).

Visual SM (iconic memory) holds information for half a second before it fades. Acoustic SM (echoic memory) lasts for around two seconds. SM has a large capacity, but most information fades too quickly to be processed (Sperling, 1960).

How do the stores work together?

The stores in the model function in a **linear** process (i.e. one-way), with information being transferred from one store to the next. Information coming in through the senses is placed briefly in the sensory store. If **attention** is paid to information in SM, it enters STM. There, according to the model, information which is **rehearsed** is then **encoded to LTM**. Information is therefore remembered in the long term only if it is rehearsed in STM.

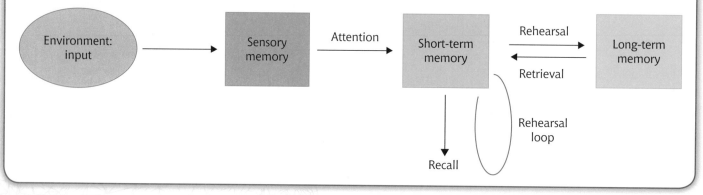

Research evidence

The **primacy effect** is where items from the start of a list are better remembered in comparison to the items in the middle, and the **recency effect** is where later items are better remembered. This supports the idea of two separate stores. Glanzer and Cunitz (1966) suggested that the primacy effect is due to **rehearsal of early items** which are then encoded into LTM, and recency due to recall of the later items which are **still in STM**.

Craik and Tulving (1975) showed that information was better recalled if questions were asked about its meaning (e.g. 'is it alive?') than about its appearance (e.g. 'is it in capital letters?'). This goes against the MSM, as it shows that **meaning** (not just rehearsal) can affect encoding to LTM.

Morris *et al*. (1985) showed that people with prior knowledge of football performed better at STM recall of football scores. This suggests that LTM can influence the performance of STM – evidence against a **one-way** transfer of information as proposed by the multi-store model.

Neurological evidence from brain scans and patients with brain damage has also supported the idea that STM and LTM are separate.

Evaluation

Top Tip

Research evidence from the previous subtopic ('The nature of memory') could support an answer on the MSM.

- The MSM idea of separate STM and LTM is well supported, for example by the **primacy** and **recency** effects.
- On the negative side, the model is too simplistic, as both STM and LTM are actually composed of several components.
- Research shows that the LTM can influence processing and that rehearsal does not always lead to LTM encoding (see above).
- The model also presents STM as a **passive** store; it is now thought that STM (or 'working memory') is involved in the active processing of information.

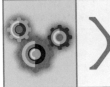

| MSM – multi-store model | SM – sensory memory | Attention |
| Rehearsal | Linear | Passive |

Quick Test 8

1. Which memory store does information reach first?
2. Name two research studies which cast doubt on the multi-store model.

The working memory model

In the early 1970s, researchers Alan Baddeley and Graham Hitch tried to replace the MSM, which they saw as limited and inaccurate. Their model, the **working memory model** (WMM, or just WM), describes the functioning of short-term memory in terms of **active processing** (Baddeley and Hitch, 1974). This means that it is seen as a system for solving problems and carrying out tasks, not merely a memory 'store' in the traditional sense. The term 'working' memory was chosen to highlight this change in emphasis.

A key feature of the model is that a **central executive (CE)**, based on **attention**, controls the other parts of the model, known as **slave systems**. The slave systems process different types of information. This allows two different tasks to be completed at once, if enough attention is available.

Top Tip

To help understand how the WMM represents the real world, think of a situation where you have had to divide your attention between different tasks. Such examples can be used in exam answers.

Overview of the model

Working memory is much more **flexible** than MSM: it is not linear because information can travel between slave systems and the CE.

Processing time is based on **real time** to do tasks. For example, how long a sentence takes to process in your head is equal to the time it would take to say the sentence. Following a pattern in your head takes as long as it would take to trace your finger round it.

The **articulatory process** is like an 'inner voice' which is responsible for rehearsing words or numbers inside your head. It has a capacity of around two seconds. The **phonological store** is sometimes called the 'inner ear'. The **visuo-spatial sketchpad** does routine visual processing, but is less well researched. It is sometimes known as the 'inner eye'.

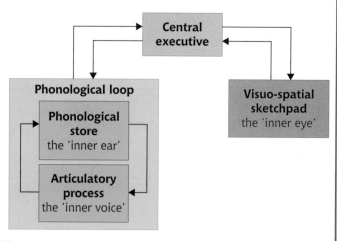

Uses and development of the model

The model has been applied to **education**. Gathercole and Baddeley (1990) studied a group of children with a language disorder, and found that their difficulties were due to a deficit in the phonological store. Understanding the nature of a child's educational problems is central to treating them in an effective way.

The model continues to be developed and improved; recently, a new slave system, the **episodic buffer**, has been proposed. This aims to provide a closer link between WM and LTM.

Key features of WMM

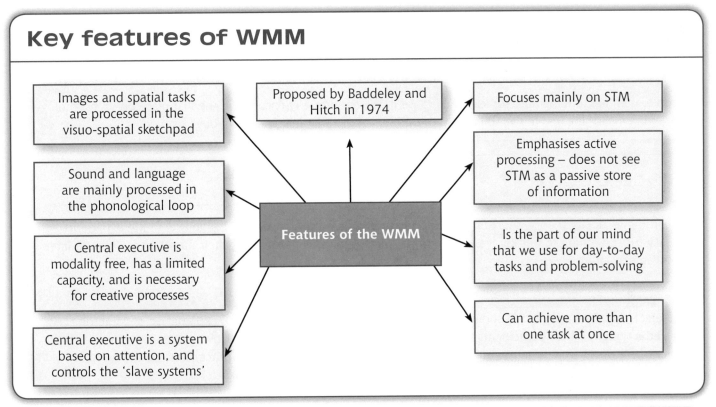

Images and spatial tasks are processed in the visuo-spatial sketchpad

Sound and language are mainly processed in the phonological loop

Central executive is modality free, has a limited capacity, and is necessary for creative processes

Central executive is a system based on attention, and controls the 'slave systems'

Proposed by Baddeley and Hitch in 1974

Features of the WMM

Focuses mainly on STM

Emphasises active processing – does not see STM as a passive store of information

Is the part of our mind that we use for day-to-day tasks and problem-solving

Can achieve more than one task at once

Research into WMM

Baddeley *et al.* (1973) asked participants to trace a 'hollow letter F' with a pointer. This was done at the same time as a verbal task without harming performance on either task. However, when participants tried to do two visual tasks at the same time, performance dropped significantly. The researchers concluded that a verbal and a spatial task can be done at the same time without much interference, as they involve separate **slave systems**.

Baddeley *et al.* (1975) found that rather than being simply limited to seven items, the number of words which could be held in STM depended on the length of the word – the longer the words, the fewer people could retain. They concluded that the phonological loop has a limited capacity based on two seconds of pronunciation time, meaning that longer words take up more space. This became known as the **word length effect**.

Evaluation of WMM

The model has been able to integrate a large number of research findings such as the word length effect, and give a more detailed picture of STM. It has been usefully applied in education and language development, for example by Gathercole and Baddeley (1990).

A weakness of the model is that the function and capacity of the CE is unclear: we don't know how much it can hold, how it manages to be modality free, or even if there is only one CE (Eysenck, 1986).

Quick Test 9

1. Which part of WM deals with verbal information?

Forgetting

People often fail to remember something because it was not properly encoded in the first place but in psychology, forgetting means the loss of the ability to retrieve information that has previously been learned.

Trace decay

According to **decay** theory, short-term memories simply fade through **time**. This links with life experience – it is easy for something to quickly leave our minds, such as when a person says their name, and a minute later you can't recall it.

Research	Evaluation
Peterson and Peterson (1959) showed 'trigrams' of letters (e.g. TBX) to participants who then had to count backwards from a number in 3s (e.g. '567, 564, 561 …') to distract them. Results suggested that information typically decays from STM within 30 seconds.	Decay is a more useful explanation of forgetting in STM than in LTM. However, the Peterson research does not rule out **displacement** by the numbers in the distraction task.

Displacement

The STM has a **limited capacity** (Miller, 1956) and therefore if new information is put in, old information has to be pushed out. Displacement is when items are forgotten because they are pushed out of a limited space. A typical analogy is squeezing a book onto one end of a small bookshelf – only for another book to fall off the other end!

Research	Evaluation
In Waugh and Norman's (1965) study, students were read a list of numbers, after which one number was repeated (this was called the 'probe' digit). Participants had to recall the number which came after the probe in the list. Numbers which came **later in the list** were recalled far better, supporting the displacement theory of forgetting. If this difference was due to decay then reading the numbers faster should have improved performance, but this was found to make only a slight difference.	Waugh and Norman's study usefully distinguishes between decay and displacement. However, displacement is based on an outdated concept of STM as a passive, unitary store.

Top Tip

You will probably have to explain **two** theories of forgetting in a single answer – ensure you know about all four.

Interference

LTM seems to be susceptible to **interference** between similar items. Unlike a computer, the human mind struggles to store very similar pieces of information without getting them confused.

Retroactive interference is where new information interferes with old, such as finding it hard to remember your old phone number after you have memorised a new one. **Proactive interference** is when old information interferes with new information, such as looking in the drawer where something *used* to be kept.

Research	Evaluation
Baddeley and Hitch (1977) studied rugby players' recall of a season's fixtures. Some players had taken part in fewer games due to injury. It was found that those players had a better recall of the fixtures they had played – presumably because there were fewer games to confuse. They had not experienced so much interference in their LTM.	Experts in a subject should suffer from interference, but in fact having a high level of knowledge seems to make it easier to take in new information. As a natural experiment, Baddeley and Hitch (1977) is uncontrolled.

Cue-dependent forgetting

In LTM, it may happen that memories are stored accurately but cannot be retrieved – it is somehow difficult or impossible to bring the information to mind. The information is stored in memory, but **retrieval failure** occurs if there is no **cue** to bring the information to mind. The term for this is **cue-dependent forgetting**.

Research	Evaluation
The tip-of-the-tongue phenomenon is where people are sure that they know something but cannot recall it. Giving a cue such as the first letter of the word is often enough to help people retrieve it (Brown and McNeill, 1966).	This theory cannot account for all cases of forgetting, but the importance of cues is well supported by research, and can be usefully applied to study skills. In your revision, use keywords as cues to help avert forgetting!

Top Tip

Ensure that you know which theories of forgetting apply to STM and which to LTM.

Top Tip

Evidence of amnesia from brain damage or drug use could also be used in answers on this subtopic.

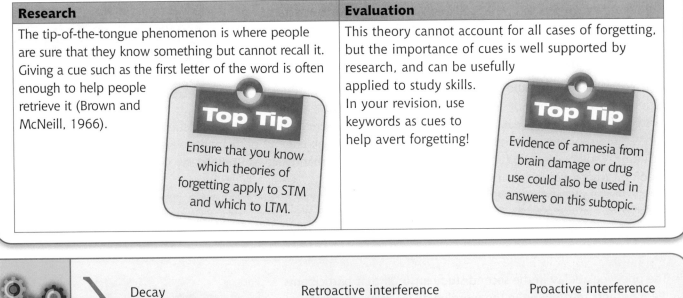

Decay	Retroactive interference	Proactive interference
Displacement	Retrieval failure	Cue

Quick Test 10

1. Which type of STM forgetting did Waugh and Norman (1965) find to be more important?
2. Which type of interference involves old information interfering with new?

Eyewitness testimony

What is eyewitness testimony?

Eyewitness testimony (EWT) is the study of memory as applied to police and legal situations, where the report of an **eyewitness** and their **memory of a crime** can be of vital importance.

Memory distortions

Sir Frederick Bartlett was one of the first to study **distortions** in LTM. He found that when his experimental participants tried to remember stories from other cultures, unfamiliar elements were **simplified**, **omitted**, or made **more familiar** (Bartlett, 1932). It became clear that a memory is not always an accurate record of what was seen or heard.

Experiments into eyewitness testimony

Loftus and Palmer (1974) showed film clips of car accidents to 45 student participants and then asked them several questions. The wording of one question was changed for each of five experimental conditions, as follows:

– 'About how fast were the cars going when they **hit** each other?'

– 'About how fast were the cars going when they **smashed** into each other?'

The other key words used were 'collided', 'bumped' and 'contacted'. Highest speed estimates came in the 'smashed' condition with a mean of 40·8 mph; the lowest estimates came in the 'contacted' condition, with a mean of 31·8 mph.

In a second part of the study, 150 participants were shown another car accident clip. One group of 50 participants were asked 'How fast were the cars going when they hit each other?', the second group were asked the same question except with '... smashed into ...' and the third were not asked about speed. One week later all participants were asked questions, including 'Did you see any broken glass?' They were more than twice as likely to say yes in the 'smashed' condition (there was in fact no broken glass).

Evaluation of Loftus and Palmer

The one-week delay in the second study ensured that participants were not just responding to the wording of the original question, and suggested that **information supplied after an event** can become part of our memory of the event.

Loftus and Palmer's research was a carefully-controlled lab study. The results have influenced police forces; many now use the **cognitive interview**, a type of questioning which aims to avoid misleading witnesses by asking them to recall events from different perspectives (Geiselman et al., 1985).

However, Yuille and Cutshall (1986) found that EWT is more accurate in the case of a real-world crime.

Factors in EWT

There are several factors that can affect whether an eyewitness remembers an event accurately.

The main **factors in eyewitness testimony** can be summarised as follows:

Information after the event – leading questions or information suggested during interviews – Loftus and Palmer (1974)
Social pressure – Asch (1951) showed that people will state a wrong answer just because other people do so. (See also page 64.)
Expectations – Bartlett (1932) research
External appearance – the appearance of a suspect, e.g. clothing, age and ethnicity, can influence judgements.

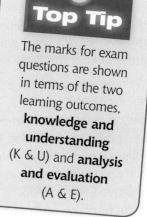

Top Tip

Structure an exam answer on **factors in EWT** around these four; use the mnemonic 'I see' (I, S, E and E from the points listed) to help remember them. Include short research summaries.

 With Social Psychology and the study of Law.

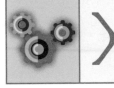

EWT – eyewitness testimony	Questioning	Expectations
Crime	Social pressure	Cognitive interview

Sample exam questions

1. Explain the three processes in memory, referring to research evidence. (6, 4)
2. Discuss the features of STM and LTM. (6, 4)
3. Describe and evaluate the working memory model. (8, 4)
4. Discuss two types of forgetting which relate to LTM. Support your answer with research evidence. (8, 4)
5. Describe and evaluate a research study into EWT. (4, 4)

Top Tip

The marks for exam questions are shown in terms of the two learning outcomes, **knowledge and understanding** (K & U) and **analysis and evaluation** (A & E).

Quick Test 11

1. What was the difference between the two Loftus and Palmer studies?
2. What are the factors which affect EWT?

Stress and biological psychology

What is stress?

The term **stress** is used on a daily basis to explain people's behaviour. If a friend shouts at you shortly before an exam, you might say they are 'stressed'. Stress is both a psychological and a biological process.

Biological psychology

Biological psychology aims to link psychology with the biological processes in the human body. Of particular importance is the **nervous system** – the network of **neurons** (nerve cells or brain cells) which control our actions. The nervous system has two parts – the **central nervous system** (CNS), comprising the brain and spinal cord, and the **peripheral nervous system** (PNS), the nerves which connect the brain to other areas of the body. Biological psychology also states that the structure of our bodies, including the nervous system, is a result of **evolution by natural selection** as first proposed by Charles Darwin.

The fight-or-flight response

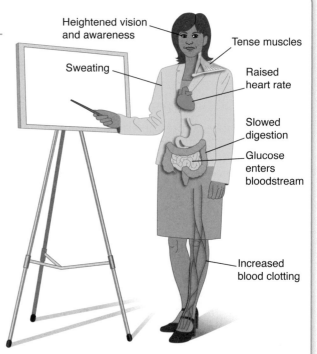

Heightened vision and awareness

Sweating

Tense muscles

Raised heart rate

Slowed digestion

Glucose enters bloodstream

Increased blood clotting

The **fight-or-flight response** (also called the 'acute stress response') is the body's immediate reaction to a threatening situation. This could happen if you are in a fight, feel threatened, or even if you have to give a speech. Changes in our bodies during fight-or-flight are shown in the diagram.

Walter Cannon (1927) came up with the theory of the 'fight-or-flight' response. The key idea is that an animal or person reacts to an immediate **threat** by releasing **energy** and preparing for action – either self-defence ('fight') or running away ('flight'). No matter which option is taken, the body will benefit from energy and oxygen to the muscles, improved vision, reduced tendency to bleed, etc. Because this is the response to an immediate threat, certain longer-term processes can be switched off, for example **digestion**, as immediate survival is much more important.

Top Tip

In the modern world, the fight-or-flight response is often unhelpful, for example sweating and trembling when you have to give a speech.

The **environment of evolutionary adaptiveness** (EEA) means the environment in which human ancestors are thought to have lived for most of the evolution of our species. It is thought that humans evolved in the African savannah, and lived in small tribes of **hunter-gatherers** for approximately two million years. It is only in the last 10 000 years that we have developed agriculture and lived in settled villages and towns. This helps to explain why the stress response can be unhelpful in the modern world.

Analysis

- This response evolved in our evolutionary past to aid survival. It helps to explain why our heart rate rises and we release energy in response to threats.
- The response is an over-generalisation. Animals such as cats respond differently in a fight, and some animals such as snakes use a 'play dead' strategy in response to a threat.
- The response only covers immediate threats, and doesn't explain prolonged stress.

Two stress responses

What causes the fight-or-flight response to happen? Underlying the stress response are two key processes.

The sympathetic adrenal-medullary (SAM) system

This process involves the **autonomic nervous system** (ANS), the branch of the PNS which controls the automatic processes of our organs. This has two branches – the **sympathetic** branch, which takes control when the body is stressed or active, and the **parasympathetic** branch, which takes control when the body is at rest. When the body is stressed, nerves from the sympathetic branch of the ANS stimulate the centre of the adrenal glands (the **adrenal medulla**) to release **adrenalin** – the hormone which is most closely associated with symptoms of the fight-or-flight response, such as raised heart rate.

The HPA axis

The second process which causes the fight-or-flight response is the action of the **endocrine system**, the body's network of **glands** which release **hormones**. This system is regulated by an area of the **midbrain** called the **hypothalamus**. In stress, the hypothalamus instructs the pituitary gland to release a hormone called ACTH, which in turn instructs the **adrenal cortex** (the outside of the adrenal glands) to release stress hormones such as **cortisol**. These hormones help to release the energy needed to fight stress, and trigger the changes in the body which cause the fight-or-flight response. This set of processes is called the hypothalamic-pituitary-adrenal (HPA) axis.

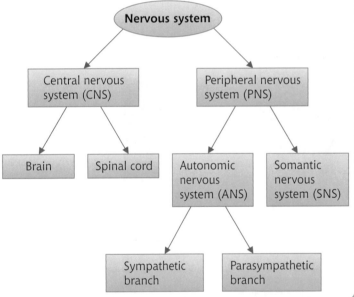

Analysis

Both of these processes happen when we are under stress, and both help to release energy. The ANS-controlled system is quicker, because hormones take effect more slowly. It is therefore particularly important in fight-or-flight situations. The HPA axis takes effect more slowly, and is important in resisting prolonged ('chronic') stress.

Top Tip

It is not necessary to evaluate these biological processes.

Quick Test 12

1. Name five biological changes which occur during fight-or-flight.
2. What are the two biological systems which trigger the fight-or-flight response?

The general adaptation syndrome

Hans Selye is the founder of the modern day study of stress. He was the first to use the term 'stress' in the psychological sense – before it had only been used in subjects such as engineering (such as the stress a train places on a bridge). Selye believed that stress could lead to illness, but that some stress could be a positive thing.

Research on rats

Selye (1936) subjected rats to a number of different stressors, including surgical injury, extremes of temperature and injections of various substances. The animals showed three key symptoms:

- enlargement of **adrenal glands**
- **ulcers** in the stomach or gut
- shrinking of the **lymph** (white blood cell) production system.

After 6–48 hours of treatment, these symptoms disappeared. However, after a further one to three months of the same treatment, symptoms returned and the animals became vulnerable to disease.

Top Tip

Read Selye (1936) online at http://neuro.psychiatryonline.org/cgi/content/full/10/2/230a

Because the response to all stressors was the same, Selye concluded that the body has a general 'stress' response to all threats, with three stages (based on his finding that the physiological triad appeared, subsided and then reappeared).

Hans Selye's research is fundamental to our modern day understanding of stress. However, **research on animals** is not always applicable to humans, as it does not take account of the **cognitive** processes involved in assessing a threat. Unlike human stress, most of the stimuli used in this experiment involved direct physical injury.

Background to the GAS

A medical doctor by training, Selye believed that the changes his rats experienced were an example of the way all animals, including humans, react to stressors such as viruses. The response was presented as a syndrome (a group of symptoms that appear together) called the **general adaptation syndrome (GAS)**.

The reaction to stress is called **adaptation**, for Selye believed that the process is an important part of how an individual learns to cope with environmental challenges.

Top Tip

When describing the alarm stage, don't forget to include some details from your knowledge of the fight-or-flight response.

Adaptation has three main stages:

1. **Alarm**: the body's reactions are heightened and a 'fight-or-flight' reaction is experienced. Internally, the adrenal glands enlarge, and stomach ulcers may be present. The immune system is damaged, with a shrinking of the lymph (white blood cell) system.

2. **Resistance**: if the stressor persists, the organism attempts to find some way of coping. Stress hormones such as cortisol are released, and the body obtains energy by burning fats. Even though the stressor is still present, symptoms from the alarm stage disappear, as the body begins to adapt.

3. **Exhaustion**: if the stress is prolonged for weeks without being overcome, the body may become exhausted. Symptoms from the first stage reappear. Ultimately this results in 'diseases of adaptation' such as heart disease, and psychological problems such as depression are also likely.

Top Tip

The resistance stage tends to be least well-explained in the exam – because on the surface, not much is happening! Write a 50-word summary of this stage in your notes.

Evaluation

The GAS is a detailed biological theory of stress, based on a large body of experimental evidence. However, a lot of the research was done on animals such as rats and birds, making it harder to apply to humans. The theory is based on sound knowledge of biological systems. However, it does not always take account of psychological factors. The idea that all organisms react to all stressors in the same way is an oversimplification.

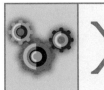

Adaptation   Alarm
Resistance   Exhaustion

Quick Test 13

1. When did the symptoms of the alarm stage disappear in Selye's rats?

Sources of stress and the transactional model

Environmental sources of stress

The term 'stress' usually refers to the **response** to a stressor. The term **stressor** is used to describe the things that cause people stress. These can be categorised into three types:

Type of stressor	Examples	
Environmental stressors	Noise, overcrowding	
Social stressors	Arguments, divorce	
Occupational stressors	Workload, deadlines	

Top Tip

Look at the other research studies in this topic for more examples of environmental stressors, such as the extremes of temperature in Selye's (1936) study.

Putting stressors into categories is a generalisation, as there is a lot of overlap between the three types. For example, arguing with a noisy neighbour is both environmental and social.

The social readjustment scale

Rahe *et al.* (1970) studied the many stressors which affect people. They believed that **social readjustment** was a key factor in stress, as people have to alter their lifestyles to accommodate changes. Their analysis included both negative items such as a jail term and positive ones such as a new job. They showed that the more stressors a person experiences, the greater their level of ill health. However, the connection was weak, perhaps because it didn't allow for individual perceptions.

Analysis

Different types of stress tend to have a very similar effect on the body, and what matters is the number of stressors experienced and the way we perceive them. In a lab experiment, Glass *et al.* (1969) showed that noise leads to stress, but has the biggest effect when it is unpredictable. This shows that **expectations** play a major role in whether we get stressed.

Rahe's research acts as if stressors affect us in a direct way, the way the weight of a lorry impacts on a bridge. This is known as the **engineering model** of stress. However, human reaction to stress is complex, and this model is now seen as inaccurate.

Top Tip

Pin research summaries around your study space, on note cards or post-its: name, researcher, findings, evaluation point(s).

Sources of stress and the transactional model

The transactional model

The engineering model assumes that everyone reacts in the same way to stressors. Some things, like being attacked by a bear, would lead to a fight-or-flight response in anyone, but most stressors are not so clear cut. For example, some people find exams overwhelmingly stressful, but others do not get worked up about them.

According to the **transactional model** of Lazarus and Folkman (1984), stress depends very much on the **perceptions** of the individual. In this model, how people react to stressors is seen as a three-stage cognitive process.

- **Primary appraisal**: This is where a stressor is assessed and the individual determines whether it is a threat or not.
- **Secondary appraisal**: This is where the person assesses their own ability to cope; for example, by deciding if they are feeling full of energy or tired.
- **Coping methods**: This is where strategies to deal with the stress are implemented. These can be taught – we can learn to cope better with the stress which we experience.

According to this model, the reason for getting stressed is because of a mismatch between the **perceived threat** level and our **perceived ability to cope**.

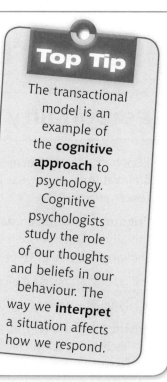

Top Tip

The transactional model is an example of the **cognitive approach** to psychology. Cognitive psychologists study the role of our thoughts and beliefs in our behaviour. The way we **interpret** a situation affects how we respond.

Evaluation of the transactional model

This is the most popular model of stress today, and is the first to include **cognitive** aspects of stress.

The model has led to a huge growth in interest in stress-reduction strategies, through the understanding that reducing stress lies not just in changing your environment but also in changing your thoughts.

However, the role of cognition in managing stress is limited. Even if we feel that we can cope and even enjoy certain stressors, some will still produce the fight-or-flight response in the body.

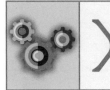

Stressor

Engineering model

Primary and secondary appraisal

Social readjustment

Transactional model

Cognitive

Quick Test 14

1. What happens in the secondary appraisal stage?

Individual differences in stress

Personality

Personality factors seem to play a major role in the way people respond to stress, and this can affect health. Survival from cancer has been found to depend partly on psychological characteristics such as 'fighting spirit' (Greer *et al.*, 1979).

Friedman and Rosenman (1974) conducted an eight-year study of over 3000 American men aged 39–59. Initially, by means of an interview and questionnaire, they were classified as showing 'type A' or 'type B' behaviour.

- Type As showed time-urgency, excessive competitiveness and controlled hostility.

- Type Bs were easy-going, ambitious in a relaxed way and much less hostile.

- The longitudinal study showed that type A men were more than twice as likely to develop coronary heart disease and that, even taking other risk factors into account, they were still twice as likely to have a heart attack when compared to type Bs.

> **Top Tip**
>
> The term '**individual differences**' in psychology usually refers to **inherent** differences between people, such as their age and sex, not temporary differences in their situation such as a stressful job.

Evaluation

Friedman and Rosenman's study was the first to show that a psychological trait could be a **risk factor** in heart disease, just like smoking or a bad diet. It was a large-scale, well-designed study.

However, the participants were all male, making it unclear whether results apply to women. Ivancevich and Matteson (1980) suggested that, rather than being a personality trait, type A behaviour depended on the fit between the person and the environment.

A follow-up study 22 years later found a much smaller difference. However, it could be that in their later years, type A men stopped being so hostile and competitive.

Age

The type of stressors we suffer from, and the extent to which we cope with them, vary with age. Colten and Gore (1991) found that teenagers exhibit stress symptoms more than adults. The elderly also experience stressors very strongly.

Another effect of age is that the type of stressors which people suffer from will also vary. Young people may be stressed by exams and relationships, while older people are more likely to experience stress from health problems and bereavement.

Sex

There are considerable sex differences in stress. Males and females differ biologically, with men having a greater and more sustained release of **adrenalin** when a stressor is experienced (Frankenhauser *et al.*, 1976).

The way a person reacts to the stress hormone **cortisol** may also depend on sex. Taylor *et al.* (2000) found that the hormone **oxytocin** can reduce cortisol. Oxytocin is affected by sex hormones: it is boosted by oestrogen, whereas testosterone makes it less effective.

Heart attacks are much more common among males, and while lifestyle is partly responsible for this, Friedman and Rosenman's research (above) suggests that personality also plays a role.

Thinking style

The **transactional model** of stress discussed in the previous subtopic shows how thinking style can affect our stress levels. Therapy to reduce stress often focuses on changing people's attitudes towards their stressors.

Locus of control means a person's perception of whether or not they are in control of events. A high **internal** locus of control means that a person views themselves as in charge of their own life, while a high **external** locus of control means that they see their fate as being out of their own hands (Rotter, 1966). Johnson and Sarason (1978) found that people with a high external locus of control were more likely to suffer from anxiety due to stressful life events.

> **Top Tip**
>
> Use the mnemonic 'PAST' to remember these four factors in individual differences – personality, age, sex and thinking style.

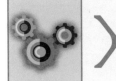

Individual differences	Personality	Age
Sex	Thinking style	

Quick Test 15

1. Name one sex difference in stress.

Health effects of stress

Short-term effects

Short-term stress is also called **acute stress**. Due to the physical nature of the fight-or-flight response, stress can produce effects on health even in the short term (i.e. anything from minutes up to a few days). The person is likely to sweat profusely, feel tense and have difficulty sleeping.

The fight-or-flight syndrome can initially boost the immune response, but stress soon begins to have a negative effect on the immune system. The body is more likely to suffer from infections and viruses – Cohen *et al.* (1991) found that high-stress individuals were more **susceptible** to the common cold. This may be because the GAS leads to shrinkage of the **lymph system**, the parts of the body which produce white blood cells. In a natural experiment, Kiecolt-Glaser *et al.* (1984) showed that students had reduced levels of white blood cells at exam time.

Acute stress will also affect mental health – the person may anger easily, and be moody and irritable. This will be shown in behaviour such as emotional outbursts. They may dwell on the stressor and have difficulty concentrating on other tasks.

Top Tip

Do not forget about short-term effects on **mental health**. It may help to think of them in three categories: subjective (e.g. feeling tense and angry), behavioural (e.g. emotional outbursts) and cognitive (e.g. difficulty concentrating).

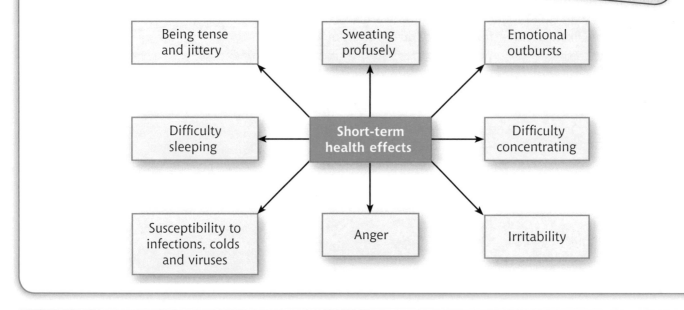

Make the link with Biology and Medicine.

Long-term effects

Long-term stress is usually called **chronic stress**. As stress lasts longer, health effects tend to become more serious, and can cause lasting damage. People are likely to suffer from what Selye (1956) called **diseases of adaptation**, such as heart disease. Appearance can be affected, with skin conditions such as psoriasis likely to worsen when a person is stressed.

Psychologically, a person's mood is likely to suffer, leaving them prone to **anxiety** and even **depression**. Stress can be a **triggering factor** in a number of mental illnesses, including **schizophrenia** and **eating disorders**. Mumford et al. (1991) found that among Asian girls in the UK, those who were most traditional in their dress and outlook were more susceptible to eating disorders, perhaps because of a greater 'culture clash' making life more stressful.

Brady (1958) showed that 'executive' monkeys developed stomach ulcers when given a task requiring constant vigilance to avoid shocks. If the monkey failed to press a button within 20 seconds, a shock was delivered. A control group showed that it was the stress of the task, not the shocks themselves, which led to the ulcers.

In humans, this may link to jobs which require focused attention for long periods. When Johansson et al. (1978) studied workers in a Swedish sawmill, they found that one group of workers had high levels of responsibility and a monotonous task (the stage of finishing/processing the timber which was monotonous but important). They also worked in social isolation. These workers were found to have raised levels of stress hormones, and to take more days off sick than a control group.

Top Tip

In the exam, you can pick up A & E marks by providing research evidence to support your knowledge. Studies throughout this topic relate to health, so there is a wealth of research for you to draw on.

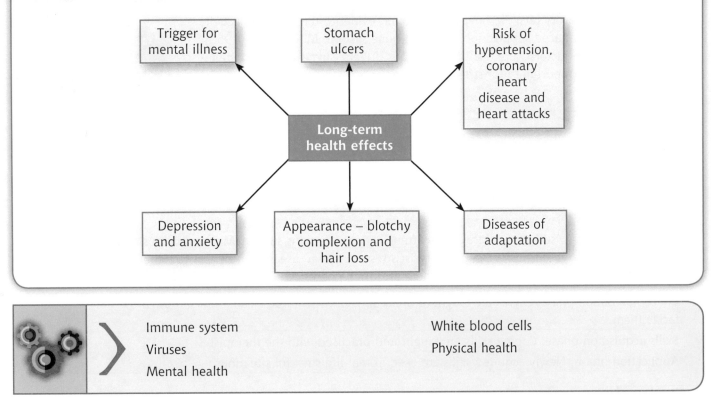

Immune system   White blood cells

Viruses   Physical health

Mental health

Quick Test 16

1. Name a short-term mental health effect of stress.

Stress management strategies

What is stress management?

There are several ways of tackling stress. These can be divided into **physiological techniques** – ways of tackling the body's physical response; **coping strategies** – ways that an individual can change the way they think about or approach stressors; **social support** – using friends and family to reduce stress; and **time management** – altering behaviours and routines in order to reduce stressors, e.g. in the workplace.

Physiological techniques – exercise

In our evolutionary past, the fight-or-flight response would have been followed by immediate physical exertion, and health problems can result from failing to metabolise **glucose** (blood sugar) released during the response. Exercise can help to do this, and is also thought to reduce the activity of the sympathetic branch of the ANS.

Evaluation

In a study of laboratory rats, Fleshner (2000) found evidence that physical activity can reduce stress-induced suppression of the immune system. Morris *et al*. (1953) found that bus conductors were healthier than bus drivers, suggesting that active careers give more opportunity for stress reduction.

Individual coping strategies – SIT

There are a great variety of **relaxation techniques**, such as **meditation**, which can prove helpful for dealing with day-to-day stress.

In more severe cases, sufferers of stress may attend therapy sessions such as Meichenbaum's **stress inoculation therapy**. This trains people to resist stressors (like a disease can be resisted after a vaccination), using role-play, visualisation and practice. There are three phases:

Conceptualisation phase: Clients are taught to break stressors down into smaller units in order to tackle them.
Skills acquisition phase: Coping skills are taught and practised with the therapist.
Application phase: Newly acquired skills are used in real-life stressful situations.

Evaluation

SIT can be effective and long lasting (Meichenbaum, 1977). It deals with the causes of stress, and teaches practical strategies. However, the therapy sessions can be time-consuming and expensive.

Social support

A person's social network plays a key role in stress reduction. Nuckolls *et al.* (1972) found that for pregnant women with high stress levels, those with good levels of social support were far less likely to experience pregnancy complications than those without (91% compared to 33%). There are cultural differences in social support – Kim and McKenry (1998) found that ethnic minorities in the USA used their parents or children for social support more than white Americans did.

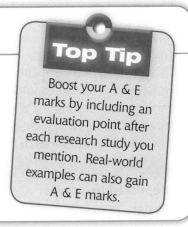

Evaluation

Social support from a partner has been shown to benefit health (Tache *et al.*, 1979). A weakness of this strategy is that many people who lack social support also lack the confidence or skills to develop their social network.

Time management

Leaving essential tasks to the last minute can increase stress levels. Time management can help a person make better use of their time, and avoid problems such as the **planning fallacy** – the tendency to underestimate task-completion times (Buehler *et al.*, 1994).

One approach to time management in the workplace is the **ABC analysis**, i.e. taking a task list and rating items A, B or C according to how important they are. Another is a **Pareto analysis**. This is based on the assumption that 80% of tasks take 20% of work time. These simpler tasks should be prioritised, thus getting the bulk of the work done quickly.

Evaluation

Time management skills are easy to teach and can be of great benefit – but only for dealing with certain stressors. Some stressors are unexpected and can't be planned for.

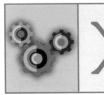

Physiology	Social support	Stress inoculation therapy
ABC analysis	Pareto analysis	Planning fallacy

Sample exam questions

1. Describe and evaluate the general adaptation syndrome. (8, 4)
2. Discuss the role of individual differences in stress. (8, 4)
3. Describe and evaluate one stress reduction strategy. (4, 4)

Top Tip

Boost your A & E marks by including an evaluation point after each research study you mention. Real-world examples can also gain A & E marks.

Quick Test 17

1. What are the phases of SIT?
2. What is the planning fallacy?

Experiments

Experiments aim to study the effect of one **variable** on another. A variable can be any part of behaviour (e.g. heart rate), or any stimulus that affects behaviour (e.g. noise).

An experiment is a highly controlled research method. It involves changing one variable and **keeping everything else the same** (as far as possible) in order to study **cause-and-effect** between the two variables. These are called:

- The IV – **independent variable** (the variable which is changed)
- The DV – **dependent variable** (the variable which is measured)

Conditions of the IV

An experiment **randomly allocates** participants to experimental **conditions**. There must be at least two conditions of an IV, so that a comparison can be made between them.

The conditions are determined by the IV – one for each value of the variable. For example, to test the effect of caffeine on memory, an experimenter could give one group of participants a high level of caffeine and another group zero caffeine. This comparison would have two conditions – the caffeine condition and the no-caffeine condition.

Other variables

Variables other than the IV and DV are called **extraneous** variables. These can cause **random errors** in results, so should be minimised. Two types of extraneous variables are **environmental variables**, such as background noise, and **participant variables** – differences between participants, such as in intelligence.

When an extraneous variable influences one condition more than the other it is called a **confounding variable**. If the DV shows a difference between the conditions, it is impossible to know whether the IV or the confounding variable was responsible for this effect.

Design

There are three experimental **designs**, i.e. ways of allocating participants to the conditions of an experiment. Using the same participants in both conditions can lead to **order effects** – where participants do better or worse in the second condition due to practice or boredom. There may also be **demand characteristics** – participants guessing the aim of the experiment, and acting in a way that they think the researcher wants. However, using two separate groups of participants means that results will be affected by **participant variables**. A compromise is to **match** the participants in the different conditions, to make the groups as similar as possible.

Type	Description	Advantage	Disadvantage
Repeated measures design	The same participants do all conditions of an experiment	Participant variables kept to a minimum	Order effects and demand characteristics
Independent measures design	A separate group of participants in each condition	No order effects – participant only does one condition	Participant variables
Matched participants	Matching pairs/groups of participants, then dividing them between conditions	Avoids order effects and controls some participant variables	Time-consuming and not always practical to conduct

Laboratory or field?

There are two main options for where an experiment can take place:

- Laboratory (lab) experiment – in an artificial environment
- Field experiment – in the participants' normal environment (e.g. home, workplace)

Environmental variables are **controlled** in lab experiments, reducing random errors. However, using an artificial environment means that such experiments lack **ecological validity** (see subtopic 'Issues common to all methods', page 48). A field experiment is the opposite – ecological validity is high, but environmental variables are not controlled.

Other types of experiment

A **quasi-experiment** (meaning: partial experiment) lacks control over the IV but otherwise uses experimental control. The IV may be something **fixed** such as a participant's personality. This also means that participants are not randomly allocated to conditions of a quasi-experiment.

A **natural experiment** only resembles an experiment. Here, the IV is not controlled by researchers but instead occurs by chance, and is later analysed. For example, a researcher might ask students what revision strategies they had used during their Standard Grades, and then look for any effect on their exam results. With no control or random allocation, **confounding variables** cannot be ruled out.

Top Tip

Look for examples of different types of experiments throughout this book.

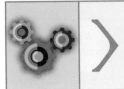

Cause-and-effect	IV – independent variable	DV – dependent variable
Random allocation	Conditions	Extraneous and confounding variables
Experimental design	Quasi-experiment	Natural experiment

Quick Test 18

1. Which design(s) use the same participants for all conditions?

The survey method

Types of survey

There are two type of survey – **interviews**, which are conducted face-to-face, and **questionnaire surveys**, which use a written list of questions. Both gather data by **asking** participants **questions**.

You will have already come across surveys in a whole range of areas but in scientific studies, such as psychological research, the design of interviews and questionnaires must be very carefully planned to avoid misleading participants or introducing **bias**.

Types of question

Either type of survey could make use of **closed questions**, or **open-ended questions**, or both.

- Closed questions provide a selection of answers (e.g. yes/no, or a set of options).
- Open-ended questions allow the respondent to say/write anything.

Many surveys include only closed questions, as these are **easier to analyse**.

QUESTIONNAIRE

Age
20 and under ☐   21–29 ☐   30–39 ☐

Favourite colour
Blue ☐   Green ☐   Red ☐

How do you feel today?
Happy ☐   Sad ☐   Not sure ☐

The questionnaire survey

A **questionnaire** is an on-screen or printed list of questions.

Typically, questionnaires in a survey are distributed to a **large sample** of participants. There are a number of ways of distributing the questionnaires, including:

- post
- internet
- email

The questionnaire must be easy for the participants to understand, as a researcher will not be there to explain it. If it is clear and accessible, people will also be more likely to complete and **return** the questionnaire.

Avoid leading questions

Avoid emotive language

Avoid jargon

Design points

Avoid ambiguity

Avoid bias

Evaluation of questionnaire surveys

Advantages	Disadvantages
• Well-designed questionnaires with closed questions are relatively quick and easy to answer and can gather a lot of data. • Answers can be analysed easily, forming totals and percentages.	• As the answers to structured questionnaires are fixed choice, they do not allow respondents to express opinions which are different from those offered. There may also be **researcher bias** in the selection of options. • Questions can't be clarified or explained to participants.

The interview survey

The key characteristic of an **interview** is that questions are asked **face-to-face**, making research more time-consuming, but allowing misunderstandings to be clarified. There are three types of interview.

An **unstructured interview** does not stick to a fixed list of questions; rather the interviewer can vary the questioning depending on how a participant responds. Many open-ended questions may be used, providing rich, detailed data. However, responses will vary widely between participants, making results hard to analyse.

A **semi-structured interview** uses a set list of questions, but allows the interviewer some freedom. The interviewer may ask the respondent to elaborate on some answers.

A **structured interview** uses a fixed list of questions. It is therefore similar to a questionnaire survey, except conducted face-to-face. The interviewer will not go beyond the questions on the list, but can make clarifications. Structured interviews are useful when interviewing a large number of participants.

Evaluation of interview surveys

Top Tip

Evaluation depends on the type of surveys/ interviews and the type of questions used. Specify which type you mean in exam answers (e.g. 'in an unstructured interview with open questions ...').

Advantages	Disadvantages
• Face-to-face format allows questions to be explained if necessary. • Unstructured interviews can be personalised to each participant and can provide rich data.	• Participants may distort the truth in order to look good to the interviewer. This is known as **social desirability bias**. • Individual interviews are costly and time-consuming to run, and the data from open questions is hard to analyse.

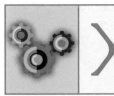

Survey	Questionnaire	Open questions
Closed questions	Bias	Structured interview
Semi-structured interview	Unstructured interview	

1. What is a closed question?

Observation

Naturalistic vs structured

A **naturalistic observation** involves simply watching and recording whatever unfolds in a natural, everyday situation. Naturalistic observation is the only method in psychology which gathers data on spontaneous behaviour **as it happens**. However, it lacks any **control** over the many variables which could influence a person's behaviour, and it is impossible to **replicate**.

An alternative is to put participants into a lab and observe them doing a task – a **structured observation**. Such observations are more controlled, but lack **ecological validity**.

Participant vs non-participant observation

In both types of observation described in the previous section, the researcher is on the outside and does not influence the situation, like a birdwatcher observing birds. This is called **non-participant observation**. In **participant observation**, one or more researchers **take part** in the social situation.

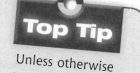

Top Tip

Unless otherwise stated, descriptions of the observation method usually refer to naturalistic, non-participant observation.

> In a classic example of a participant observation, a researcher and his colleagues pretended to be hearing voices in their heads, and were admitted to a psychiatric hospital (Rosenhan, 1973). They then took part in ordinary hospital activities, observing how the psychiatric patients were treated by hospital staff.

Participant observation gives the observer a **unique insight** into a social situation, and participants can more easily get used to their presence. However, as the researcher gets personally involved in the situation, it can become hard for them to view events objectively.

Disclosed vs undisclosed observation

Any of the types of observation described above could be **disclosed** – where participants know they are being observed – or **undisclosed** – kept secret.

Disclosing the observation has the problem that if people know they are being watched, this tends to change their behaviour. This is known as the **observer effect**. However, undisclosed observation may be **unethical**, as participants haven't given **informed consent** to take part.

Top Tip

You need to understand the strengths and weaknesses of different types of observation. Drawing a summary table in your notes will help.

One way of reducing the observer effect is to use discreetly placed **video cameras**. As cameras are less intrusive, behaviour may be more natural. It is never ethically correct to make secret observations of people in private, although some ethical codes allow observation in **public places** where people would expect to be observed by strangers (BPS, 2001), for example on a sports pitch.

Observation in experiments

Many experiments use observations as part of their procedure. However, these are not observation studies, as they manipulate an IV and record one or more numerical DV, instead of gathering a range of observational data. It is useful to remember that there is a degree of **overlap** between research methods in psychology.

Observation schedules

In some observation studies, observers use an **observation schedule** – a written list of expected behaviours. This makes recording easier, as behaviours can be ticked off each time they occur.

By providing an objective standard, observation schedules can improve the **reliability** of recordings taken by more than one observer.

Inter-observer reliability means the extent to which two observers produce the same results when looking at the same data. This is never perfect, but well-trained observers show a high level of inter-observer reliability.

Participant number	Stands up	Scratches head	Eats a snack
P1			
P2			
P3			
P4			

Evaluation of observations

Advantages	Disadvantages
• Detailed record of real-life behaviour **as it happens** • Captures behaviour in its true social **context**	• Lacks the **control** of an experiment, so cannot infer cause-and-effect relationships • Hard to **replicate** the results of an observational study, as each social situation is unique

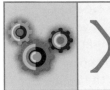

Naturalistic observation	Structured observation	Participant observation
Disclosed observation	Observer effect	Observation schedule
Inter-observer reliability		

Quick Test 20

1. Which type of observation involves watching participants in their everyday environment?
2. Give a weakness that is always true of observation.

Case-studies

A case-study is another example of a **non-experimental** research method. It is usually based on one individual **case**, but could also be conducted on a small group such as a family, team or workplace. Case-studies were famously used by Freud as he developed the psychoanalytic approach.

Features of case-studies

A case-study is usually **longitudinal**, i.e. it follows an individual or group over an extended period of time. It is an **in-depth** study where rich, detailed information is built up. This will include a **case history** – information about the person's past such as family details, education, relationships and employment. The researcher will typically gather a large amount of data using various techniques which might include **ability tests**, such as tests of IQ and memory, and **brain scans**.

Research examples

Case-studies are done for many reasons. Some of the best-known case-studies in psychology are of individuals with unique psychological problems or brain damage.

- In the study of memory, several case-studies have been conducted into the effects of brain damage on memory, such as the case of HM (Scoville and Milner, 1957).

- In the area of early socialisation, case-studies of deprived children have been useful in understanding the psychological effect of a loss/lack of an attachment bond.

- In atypical behaviour, case-studies have been conducted into patients with unusual psychological disorders.

Top Tip

Use real case-studies as examples in your exam answers – but don't waste time going into too much detail.

In the above examples, the case-study method was particularly suitable because the individuals involved were **unique** in some way.

> Thigpen and Cleckley (1954) presented a famous case of **dissociative identity disorder** (or 'multiple personality'). In their interviews with a female patient, it became apparent that she had more than one personality. One, calling herself 'Eve White', was timid and law abiding, while 'Eve Black' was self-destructive and wild. Personality tests and IQ tests confirmed the differences between the two personalities, which could be brought out through hypnosis. A third, more reasonable personality emerged through therapy. Her case was made into a film, 'The Three Faces of Eve'.

Evaluation of case-studies

Case-studies are an extremely useful, sometimes essential, tool but, as a researcher builds up a personal acquaintance with a participant, it may be hard to remain objective. It is not always possible to generalise the results of a case-study to other people.

Advantages	Disadvantages
• Essential for studying unusual cases • A source of very rich and meaningful data (it is a qualitative method) • Longitudinal study – not just a snapshot	• Time-consuming and expensive to carry out • Close relationship with participant(s) makes research less objective • Results hard to generalise and impossible to replicate

Multi-method studies

While it is usually possible to say that a study uses one method, some draw on several. A case-study will often involve one or more of the other research methods – typically, the participant will be **interviewed** and may fill in some questionnaires as well. The researcher may decide to observe the participant, using either a naturalistic observation or a structured observation.

Other **multi-method studies** include research studies where both interviews and surveys are used, observation studies where surveys are carried out, or experiments where participants later take part in a survey. Such studies are more complex, but potentially give the researcher more detailed and useful information.

Examples of multi-method studies in psychology include:

• La Pierre (1943) – observation and survey

• Ainsworth *et at*. (1978) – experiment and observation

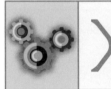

Case history	In-depth	Longitudinal
Brain scan	Ability test	Multi-method study

Quick Test 21

1. Give three characteristics of the case-study method.
2. What kind of techniques can be used to gather data in a case-study?

Correlation

Correlation is a technique used to find the **relationship** between two variables, called **co-variables**. Data are displayed on a **scattergram**.

Scattergrams

A scattergram is a graph showing one co-variable on each axis. The researcher in a correlational study obtains a score on both variables for every participant.

For example, a study could measure someone's IQ (see page 92) and use a questionnaire to find out the number of books they read per year. Each participant's scores would then be shown on the scattergram.

Top Tip

Do not use a scattergram to display experimental data.

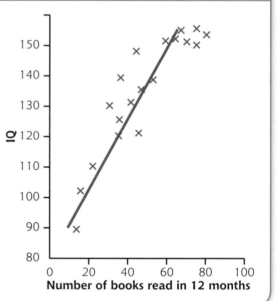

Positive and negative correlations

The pattern of points on the scattergram gives a visual impression of the relationship between the co-variables:

- If high scores on one variable tend to go with high scores on the other and the points on the graph rise from left to right there is a **positive correlation**.

- If high scores on one variable tend to go with low scores on the other and the points on the graph fall from left to right there is a **negative correlation**.

To help researchers interpret the graph, a line is drawn with the smallest possible distance between the points and the line. This is called the **line of best fit**.

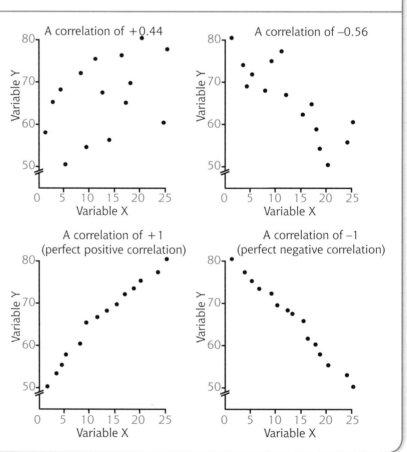

Strength

This **strength** of relationship between the co-variables is expressed on a scale ranging from − 1 (perfect negative correlation) through zero (no relationship) up to +1 (perfect positive correlation); the figure calculated to express the relationship is known as a **correlation coefficient**. For the requirements of the Higher Psychology exam, it is **not** necessary to be able to **calculate** correlation coefficients, but knowing about the concept will allow you to understand research studies.

Top Tip

Always remember that correlation shows a relationship, not cause-and-effect.

The stronger the relationship (either positive or negative), the closer points on the scattergram will be to the line of best fit. If there is no relationship at all (a **zero correlation**), the points will be scattered randomly, and it will be impossible to draw a line of best fit.

A strong correlation shows that two variables are consistently related. However, the **reason for the relationship** between the two variables in question is not always clear. **Cause-and-effect** should not be assumed. In the above example of books and IQ, it would be easy to assume that having a higher IQ **causes** people to read more books. But it is also possible that reading a lot boosts IQ, or that some third variable could affect both co-variables. Without controlled experimentation, it is impossible to know which variable is affecting which.

Top Tip

Whether a correlation is strong or weak is entirely separate from the issue of whether it is positive or negative. Do not mix up a strong correlation with a positive correlation.

Evaluation

A strong correlation enables researchers to **predict** the value of one co-variable from the value of the other, and the technique is useful in situations where experimental manipulation would be impossible. It also provides a good starting point for later experimental studies.

However, correlation establishes a relationship only, never cause-and-effect, and the relationship may be due to variables not included in the study. Correlation data tend to come from non-experimental methods (e.g. surveys), which are not always accurate.

> Look for correlational research in your other subjects, for example Geography.

> Co-variables   Scattergram   Relationship
> Correlation coefficient   Line of best fit   Positive/negative correlation
> Strong/weak correlation   Zero correlation

Quick Test 22

1. Why does a correlation not show cause-and-effect?
2. Describe a 'line of best fit'.

Issues common to all methods

Sampling

In psychology research, a **population** could mean the whole population of a country, but more often it means a specific group: for example, Scottish students. The **target population** is the population that a particular study is interested in.

Sampling means selecting **participants** from the target population. A sample should contain the same variety of people as found in that population – in other words, it should be **representative**. A good sample will also be **large** and **unbiased**.

Random	Opportunity	Volunteer/self-selecting
A **random sample** is where **every individual in a population has an equal chance of being chosen**. This could be done by drawing names from a hat or allocating computer-generated random numbers to each member of the population. Random sampling usually results in a representative sample, but is time-consuming to carry out.	An **opportunity sample** is chosen on the basis of **convenience**; for example, by asking members of your class to take part. This is usually the easiest sampling method, but suffers from bias – some members of the population may not be included.	A **volunteer** or **self-selecting** sample means that participants come forward of their own choice, perhaps responding to an advert. It is simple to arrange, but the sample may be biased towards members of the population with outgoing or helpful personalities.

WANTED
Female participants aged 20–30 for psychological experiment. Will only take 2 hours of your time and you will be paid. For more information visit www.psychology_is_fun.co.uk |

Class list: Fiona, James, Sarah, Peter, Bruce, Martin, Gillian, Jonathan

Hypotheses

A research study must state two or more **hypotheses**. These are statements of what the researchers expect to find. In an experiment, the **experimental hypothesis** states that the IV will have an effect on the DV. For example:

There will be a difference in the level of recall between participants who were shown words and participants who were shown pictures.

A **two-tailed** hypothesis, like the one above, doesn't state the direction of the difference, i.e. whether scores will rise or fall. It is best to predict a direction if you can; this is called a **one-tailed** hypothesis. For example:

Participants who were shown pictures will recall more items than participants who were shown words.

The **null** hypothesis states that the IV will **not** affect the DV, and any difference between conditions is due to **chance factors** such as participant variables. For example:

The null hypothesis is that there will be no difference between group 1 (words) and group 2 (pictures) other than random error as a result of chance factors.

Alternative and correlational hypotheses

Top Tip

You may have to suggest a hypothesis in the exam. Correlational hypotheses should never refer to the **effect** of *x* on *y*, always the **relationship** between *x* and *y*.

With a non-experimental study (e.g. a survey), the prediction is termed an **alternative hypothesis**. A null hypothesis is also used.

A **correlational hypothesis** predicts the strength and direction (negative or positive) of a correlation – usually it will predict a **strong relationship** – and the **correlational null hypothesis** will predict that there will **not** be a strongly positive/strongly negative correlation.

Ecological validity

A study which takes place in a participant's **natural environment** and involves a **realistic task** is said to have high **ecological validity**. This means that it is true to life (not artificial), making it easier to draw conclusions. However, there is often a trade-off between realism and **control**, with more tightly controlled studies having lower ecological validity.

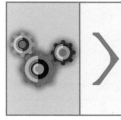

> Target population
> Representative
> Null hypothesis
> One-tailed/two-tailed

> Unbiased
> Alternative hypothesis
> Ecological validity

> Experimental hypothesis
> Correlational (null) hypothesis
> Sampling – random, opportunity, volunteer

Quick Test 23

1. Which method of sampling is least likely to produce a biased sample?
2. What is the minimum number of hypotheses a study should have?

Data analysis and graphs

Qualitative vs quantitative data

Some studies, for example surveys using open questions, produce **qualitative data**. These are non-numerical data such as descriptions.

Most studies produce **quantitative data**, i.e. data based on numbers. This data can be analysed using statistics or displayed in graphs. For convenience, quantitative data may be converted into **percentages**, i.e. standardised scores out of 100, making results easier to interpret.

Measures of central tendency

There are three **measures of central tendency** – ways of showing the **average** or most typical value of a set of data.

The mean	The **mean** is calculated by adding together all scores in a set of data and dividing by the number of values. It includes every score in the calculation. However, it can be distorted by extreme high or low scores.
The mode	The **mode** is the **most common** or popular score. This can be useful to avoid extreme values. However, some sets of data do not have a mode.
The median	The **median** is the midpoint of the data, obtained by putting scores in order, low to high, and finding the one in the centre. If there is an even number of scores, the mean of the middle two scores is calculated.

Top Tip

You will not have to do calculations in the exam – *knowledge of the concepts is all that is required.*

Measures of dispersion

Measures of central tendency alone give no indication of whether scores are generally close to or far away from the average. The purpose of **measures of dispersion** is to show how widely data are spread out.

The range	The **range** is the **difference between the lowest and highest scores**, calculated by subtracting the lowest from the highest. It is limited in that it doesn't reflect the distribution of the other data.
The standard deviation	The **standard deviation** shows the typical amount by which the scores in the distribution **differ from the mean**. The calculation is based on finding the difference between each score and the mean, and then calculating the average of these differences. An advantage is that all data are included in the calculation.

Graphs

Graphs are used to present results and also to perform a visual analysis. Some of the most common types are shown here.

Top Tip

You may have to interpret a graph in the exam, or suggest a suitable graph for a set of data.

Bar graph: y-axis % (0 to 100), x-axis Condition 1, Condition 2, Condition 3	A **bar graph** shows scores as heights on two or more separated 'bars', which often represent the different **conditions** of an experiment. It allows for an easy comparison of means.
Histogram: y-axis Frequency (0 to 100), x-axis Test score 20–39 40–59 60–79 80–99	A **histogram** looks similar to a bar graph, except for the lack of gaps between the columns. This is because a histogram shows a range of values from the same category, e.g. scores on a test. The height of the columns shows frequency.
Pie chart: Behaviour 1, Behaviour 2, Behaviour 3, Behaviour 4, Behaviour 5	A **pie chart** is **not commonly used** in psychology, but can be helpful for showing the percentages of a population which engage in a behaviour. The size of each slice represents its proportion; the total should add up to 100%. Scores on a DV such as memory test scores should **not** be presented on a pie chart.

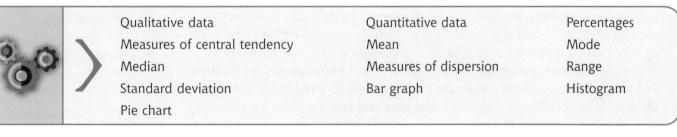

Qualitative data	Quantitative data	Percentages
Measures of central tendency	Mean	Mode
Median	Measures of dispersion	Range
Standard deviation	Bar graph	Histogram
Pie chart		

Quick Test 24

1. When is a mean not the best measure of central tendency for a set of data?

Research ethics

Researchers must follow a set of moral principles known as a **code of ethics**, which states what is and is not acceptable in research. Such codes are published by **professional organisations** such as the **BPS** (British Psychological Society). Some of the key ethical principles are described in the following sections.

Consent and briefing

Participants should give **informed consent**; consent means that they agree to take part, and being informed means that they are in full knowledge of what they are agreeing to. A **briefing** should be given, explaining what the study will entail. Participants must also be **debriefed**, meaning that the purposes of the study are explained to them at the end.

Participants have the **right to withdraw** from any study at any time, and may **retrospectively withdraw consent** when the study is over, in which case their data must be destroyed.

Top Tip

Ethics questions gain you valuable A & E marks in section 2 of the exam, but are hard to prepare for. In the exam research example, look for any obvious ethical flaws such as **deception** or **psychological harm**.

Avoiding harm

There should be no **harm** to participants, physical or mental. Their psychological wellbeing, health and dignity should be protected. While safety cannot be 100% guaranteed, the risk of harm must be **no greater than in ordinary life**.

Confidentiality

Confidentiality should be maintained. This means that results should be kept secure, and when they are published, no names or identifying information should be included.

Research on children

In the past, knowledge has been gained through ethically-dubious research on children, such as Watson and Rayner's (1920) study of 'Little Albert', where an infant was conditioned to fear an animal. However, rules are much stricter nowadays: **student researchers must not carry out experiments on children**, and professional researchers must take particular care to avoid harm and distress. Children must be willing to take part, and **parental consent** must be given on their behalf by a parent or carer.

Top Tip

If the exam research example involves child participants, you should raise the issue of **parental consent**.

Deception

Deception is where participants have been deliberately misled about the nature or purposes of a study. An example is Milgram (1963) – a study of obedience, but participants were told it was a study of memory.

Researchers should first consider any alternative procedure which could be used. If deception is essential, participants should be given full information at the earliest stage (BPS, 2001).

Top Tip

Write out your own summaries of research studies on note cards or in a computer document. Note down which subtopics each one relates to – many studies relate to more than one.

The New York subway study

Irving Piliavin and colleagues were interested in **diffusion of responsibility** – the tendency for bystanders not to help a person in need if there are other people who could help. They conducted an observational study in a public place, where an actor **faked a collapse** on a subway train in New York. Researchers hid among the bystanders, taking notes of who helped, and how quickly they helped (Piliavin *et al.*, 1969).

Ironically for a study into the unethical behaviour of strangers, there were several

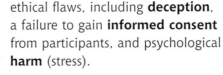

Top Tip

Knowledge of ethical limitations will gain you marks on other exam sections too, as you evaluate research examples.

ethical flaws, including **deception**, a failure to gain **informed consent** from participants, and psychological **harm** (stress).

For this study, it is vital to realise that historically, research ethics have gradually tightened up. Studies like these have helped to advance the ongoing process of deciding what is and what is not acceptable in research.

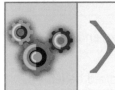

Briefing	Debriefing	Informed consent
Parental consent	Harm	Confidentiality
Deception		

Quick Test 25

1. Can children give consent to take part in a study?
2. Can participants withdraw from a study after it is finished?

The nature of prejudice

An attitude

Prejudice is a prejudgement of a person based on their appearance, or based on the groups that they are part of, such as their religion, sex or race. An **attitude** towards the person then forms, based on group characteristics, without learning about their individual traits.

Stereotypes and discrimination

A **stereotype** is a distorted view of a social group. Stereotypes can seem harmful or harmless, and may vary in how accurate they are, but are always an over-generalisation. Stereotypes are learned from society as a whole; Katz and Braly (1933) showed that even students who were not prejudiced were aware of the stereotypes of various groups.

Discrimination is prejudiced treatment of a person based on their group membership. An example might be not promoting a person in the workplace because of their race, age or sex. People may be discriminated against by an organisation's policies, even if people in that organisation are not themselves prejudiced individuals.

LaPiere (1934) found a large difference between people's **attitudes** and actual behaviour such as **discrimination** – most hotel and restaurant staff in 1930s California stated that they would not serve Asian diners, but very rarely acted on this prejudice.

Cognitive, affective and behavioural aspects

Attitudes, including prejudice, are thought to have three main components – **cognitive**, **affective** and **behavioural** (use the mnemonic 'cab' or 'abc').

The **cognitive** aspect of prejudice is the **thoughts** or beliefs a person has about an out-group. Prejudiced beliefs include stereotypes. What causes prejudiced beliefs and are they avoidable? Some psychologists think that they result from a natural tendency to oversimplify the world:

> *'Like it or not, we all make assumptions about other people, ourselves, and the situations we encounter... much of the time our expectations are functional, and indeed, we would be unable to operate without them.'* (Fiske and Taylor, 1991: 97)

The **affective** part means **feelings** about an out-group, for example fearing them, or hating them. Hatred of out-groups can lead to some of the worst examples of the **behavioural** aspects of prejudice, from attacks on minorities to genocide.

In general, the behavioural aspect of prejudice is what people actually do towards an out-group – any **actions** stemming from the prejudice, such as aggression or name-calling. This includes discrimination.

A person may show some aspects of prejudice but not others. For example, a person could think that Scottish people are stingy but not dislike them for it (cognitive but not affective), or they could hate teenagers but never act on their hatred (affective but not behavioural).

Research – confirmation bias

Once people have a stereotype, they are more likely to remember information which fits with it – thus reinforcing the stereotype for the future. This is known as **confirmation bias**.

Using student participants, Cohen (1981) identified the stereotypical features of librarians and waitresses. Participants were then shown a video, containing some information which was **consistent** with the stereotypes (e.g. the librarian had spent the day reading), and other information which was inconsistent. Recall was approximately 10% higher for information which was consistent with the stereotype.

> ### Top Tip
> Research studies in the following pages can also be used as examples of the processes of prejudice and discrimination.

This was a well-controlled experiment, but a weakness is that the student participants may have had relatively little real-world contact with librarians and waitresses, and may have responded to demand characteristics.

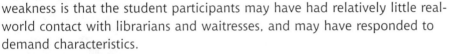

Gladwell (2005) states that attitudes to race work on two levels. A person may believe in equality on a **conscious** level, but their mind makes very fast unconscious associations which are influenced by stereotypes.

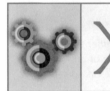

Stereotype	Prejudice	Discrimination
Bias	Cognitive	Affective
Behavioural	Confirmation bias	

Quick Test 26

1. What are the three aspects of prejudice?

Authoritarian personality theory

Two major factors help to explain social behaviour – the characteristics of the individual and the influence of the social situation. The **authoritarian personality theory** of prejudice focuses on **individual factors**.

The authoritarian personality theory draws on the **psychoanalytic approach**, which emphasises the role of **childhood** and upbringing in shaping a person's adult **personality**.

Research background

In the 1930s, Levinson and Sanford, two researchers at the University of California, conducted research which aimed to understand the roots of **anti-Semitism** (prejudice against Jewish people). They found a strong relationship between attitudes towards various **ethnic minorities** and high levels of nationalism, called 'superpatriotism'.

Adolf Hitler was an example of an authoritarian personality.

The study was broadened and, in 1950, together with psychologist Frenkel-Brunswik and sociologist Adorno, they presented the concept of the **authoritarian personality** to describe people whose traits and attitudes make them likely to develop **fascist** views, like those of Nazi leader Adolf Hitler (Adorno *et al.*, 1950).

The researchers believed that certain people develop an authoritarian personality because they have had a very **strict upbringing**, leading to them **repressing** a lot of **anger**. Because of their fear of authority, they show an exaggerated respect for conventional values, and the unconscious anger is displaced onto **weaker targets** – usually minorities in society.

Authoritarians are found to have a high level of trust for **authorities** such as the government. For example, they are more likely than average to tolerate illegal government actions (Altemeyer, 2006).

The F-scale

The research by Adorno *et al.* centred on the 'F-scale' which aimed to measure 'fascist tendencies', in particular aggressive racism and intolerance.

The scale was a list of statements which had been made by previous research participants. An example is: *'People can be divided into two distinct classes: the weak and the strong.'* Participants were given a choice of responses from 'strongly agree' to 'strongly disagree'.

Evaluation of the F-scale

A weakness of the F-scale is that all of the 'agree' options led to a higher F-score, making it hard to distinguish between people who agree with all the statements, and people who would agree to anything! This is known as **response acquiescence bias**, and Bass (1955) concluded that it had a large effect on Adorno *et al.*'s (1950) findings.

The traits

There are nine main traits which Adorno *et al.* (1950) associated with this personality type:

Conventionalism: Conventional, middle-class values	
Authoritarian submission: Submissive attitude to authority	
Authoritarian aggression: Condemnation and rejection of minorities	
Anti-intraception: Opposition to imaginative thought	
Superstition and stereotypy: Belief in fate; tendency to think in rigid categories	
Power and 'toughness': Preoccupation with strong versus weak	
Destructiveness and cynicism: Generalised hostility towards humankind	
Projectivity: Belief that wild and dangerous things go on in the world	
Sex: Exaggerated concern with sexual 'goings-on'	

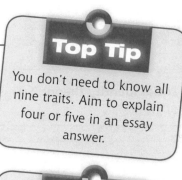

Top Tip

You don't need to know all nine traits. Aim to explain four or five in an essay answer.

Top Tip

The F-scale is a questionnaire survey, and could be given as an example in your answers on research methods.

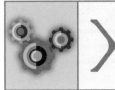

Your studies of History will help you to understand the context of this research.

Evaluation

This theory is no longer popular, with little research support for the view that a strict upbringing leads to prejudice. Altemeyer (1981) has found that of the nine authoritarian traits, only the first three (conventionalism, authoritarian submission and authoritarian aggression) **correlate** together reliably. He suggests that the term be replaced by 'RWA' – **right-wing authoritarianism**, which should be seen as an **attitude** rather than a personality type.

The theory only explains prejudice in individual cases, and struggles to explain society-wide prejudice. The F-scale suffers from response acquiescence bias, making it unreliable.

Authoritarian

Fascism

Anti-Semitism

Response acquiescence bias

Quick Test 27

1. How many authoritarian traits did Adorno *et al.* (1950) describe?
2. What does the 'F' in F-scale stand for?

Social identity theory

Social identity theory (SIT) is a theory which attempts to explain prejudice in terms of our membership of groups.

Minimal groups

Henri Tajfel was the son of a Polish-Jewish family, and most of his relatives died in the Holocaust. He enlisted in the French army, and survived as a prisoner of war by hiding his own Jewish identity. This traumatic background may have stimulated his interest in prejudice, as he developed a theory of how **personal identity** links to our membership of **social groups**.

Tajfel (1970) tried to find the **minimum requirements for discrimination** to emerge. He studied schoolboys in Bristol, dividing them into groups by asking them to choose between paintings by artists Paul Klee and Wassily Kandinsky. (The groups were actually randomised, but the boys believed this was the reason for the groupings.)

They were then set the task of giving out small cash rewards to other boys.

Despite the trivial nature of the groupings, boys gave higher rewards to in-group members. Crucially, though, the biggest factor was putting their own group ahead, even if it meant getting a lower reward overall. For example, given a choice of:

A painting by Wassily Kandinsky.

| Out-group: | 15 pence | In-group | 14 pence |
| Out-group: | 11 pence | In-group | 12 pence |

the second option was more popular – even though it meant that the overall reward was lower and the in-group member got less. Tajfel concluded that **self-esteem** rests on the success of our group(s), so people are motivated to **discriminate**, even in trivial situations. This became known as the **minimal groups** experiment.

For evaluation, note that the task was highly artificial and that the participants were young boys – not representative of the population as a whole.

Top Tip

In Tajfel's minimal group experiment, helping your group to 'win' was found to be more important than getting a bigger reward.

Social identity theory

Tajfel and Turner (1979) stated that people mentally divide the world up into 'them and us', binding up their sense of self with group membership. Then they make biased judgements, and if they perceive that the in-group is not different enough they will try to change that, possibly by harming the out-group. →

There are four main processes involved.

Social categorisation – we mentally divide the social world into groups.

Social identification – our sense of self is based on group membership, for example job or nationality. This affects self-esteem.

Social comparison – we are motivated to compare groups. These comparisons are biased towards the in-group, boosting self-esteem.

Psychological distinctiveness – we want our groups to be distinctive from and superior to other groups, and will act to increase this.

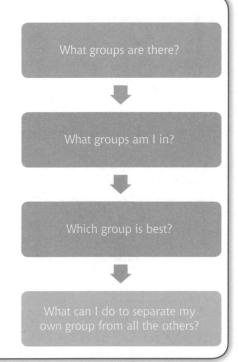

What groups are there?

What groups am I in?

Which group is best?

What can I do to separate my own group from all the others?

Evaluation

This influential theory shows that **group membership** is a vital part of who we are. The idea that our **sense of self** is based on group membership has been adopted by mainstream social psychology.

Lemyre and Smith (1985) found that people showed higher levels of self-esteem when they were allowed to discriminate between in-group and out-group members.

However, SIT's view of self-esteem as based on group membership seems simplistic, given the many other influences on self-esteem such as our skills, appearance and abilities.

Also, people who show **favouritism** towards the in-group do not always discriminate against the out-group (Brewer, 1979).

Top Tip

You need to be able to summarise the theories of prejudice, and exam questions will also expect you to support your essay answers with evaluated research evidence. You should expect to discuss **two** theories of prejudice in an essay answer.

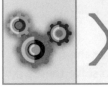

SIT – social identity theory	Social group	Discrimination
Bias	Personal identity	Minimal groups

Quick Test 28

1. Name the four processes of social identity theory.
2. Who were the participants in Tajfel's (1970) experiment?

Reducing prejudice

Ways of reducing prejudice

Psychologists want to help to **reduce** and if possible eliminate prejudice. Prejudice reduction falls into three categories:

Superordinate goals	Creating situations where members of different groups have to work together to achieve a shared goal; for example, group work, where tasks are too large to be done alone.
Education	Improving awareness of prejudice, particularly during childhood; for example, simulations/role-play of prejudice.
Contact hypothesis	The idea that prejudice will reduce when conflicting groups increase their level of contact and communication; for example, projects bringing different religious groups together.

Superordinate goals

A **superordinate goal** is a goal which is achieved with the contribution and cooperation of two or more people.

The **jigsaw technique** is where a group of people work on a task (e.g. a school project) and each group member has a key piece of information which is essential for completion of the task. This way, every member must make a contribution and it is necessary for the others to listen. The superordinate goal is the completion of the project.

Aronson and Bridgeman (1979) used the jigsaw technique in racially-mixed classrooms in Texas. They found increases in self-esteem and in liking for group members both within and across ethnic boundaries. Negative stereotypes of ethnic groups decreased among the experimental group. Academic performance also improved.

The Robber's Cave study

Muzafer Sherif (1906–88) conducted some of the most influential experiments in social psychology, and his **Robber's Cave study** is highly relevant to prejudice reduction. Sherif et al. (1954) simulated group conflict using boys on a summer camp at Robber's Cave National Park in Oklahoma. Two groups of 11 **schoolboys** were used, and all were white and middle-class – the researchers wanted them to be as similar to each other as possible.

The groups developed a strong identity, nicknaming themselves 'rattlers' and 'eagles'. They quickly came to regard the other group as **rivals**, and hostility emerged. Bringing the groups together for meals (contact hypothesis) failed to reduce hostility.

Sherif and his colleagues then faked a series of urgent problems such as the water supply failing, or the truck breaking down, thus creating superordinate goals. Boys from both groups had to work together to solve these problems and new friendships emerged. Hostility between the groups largely disappeared.

Sherif et al. concluded that prejudice can emerge from **conflict over resources** and can reduce through working together. However, as the prejudice was short term, it is very different from real-world conflicts such as those between religious groups. Also, the participants were children, making it hard to generalise the results to adults.

Education

Education involves tackling the **cognitive** aspect of prejudice. This could include:

• Raising awareness about stereotypes and discrimination.

• Teaching thinking strategies to reduce prejudiced thought processes.

Jane Elliot's 'blue eyes–brown eyes' demonstration aimed to reduce prejudice by making school children aware of how it feels to be discriminated against (Elliot, 1977). Blue-eyed and brown-eyed elementary school children took turns to receive **privileges** such as extra play time. Whichever group was on top was told by Elliot that they were better behaved and more intelligent. Prejudice spontaneously emerged, including name-calling against the out-group. Those who were being labelled as inferior did worse at a **card-sorting task**, suggesting that discrimination may harm academic performance.

Contact hypothesis

Ignorance of out-groups is often blamed for prejudice. The **contact hypothesis** states that if groups have closer contact, they will treat each other as individuals and feel less prejudiced. However, contact can also create more potential for conflict, as is often found when new groups immigrate into a country. According to Allport (1954), a key factor is **equal status contact**, in which individuals cooperate on an equal basis, without either group being superior or inferior. Ideally they will be working to achieve **superordinate goals**, in an environment structured to encourage equality and integration. Cook (1978) summarised five key factors which are essential for contact to be successful (use the acronym 'spice' to remember these):

- Support from authorities
- Personal acquaintance
- Introduction to non-stereotypical individuals
- Cooperation between groups
- Equal status

Laar *et al.* (2005) studied Dutch students who had been randomly allocated a university roommate of a different race. After sharing a room for several months, participants became less prejudiced, according to questionnaire data.

Evaluation of the strategies

Supporting research has beenlargely done on children; adult prejudices may be harder to tackle.

Supordinate goals	Education	Contact hypothesis
• Supporting research has been largely done on children; adult prejudices may be harder to tackle. • The research studies are artificial, and it may be difficult to create superordinate goals in real-world contexts.	• Elliot's technique raise awareness of prejudice and follow-up interview many years later suggested that it had long-term benefits. • Nearly everyone goes through school and is exposed to antiprejudice education, but we still live in a world with a lot of prejudice.	• Laar *et al.*'s (2005) study provides strong support, but participants (young, intelligent students) may not be representative of the whole population. • Contact alone is not enough (see Sherif *et al.*, 1954, below), so the concept of equal status contact is more useful.

Sample exam questions

1. Explain the nature of prejudice. Your answer should include cognitive, affective and behavioural aspects Include research evidence. (12, 8)

2. Discuss how education **and** the contact hypothesis can help to reduce prejudice. Support your answer with research evidence. (12, 8)

1. According to Aronson and Bridgeman, what increased when the jigsaw technique was used?
2. Name Cook's (1978) factors which make **contact** successful.

Conformity

Conformity can be defined as social pressure to change our behaviour or beliefs, in order to come into line with others in a group. Pressure to conform usually comes from your peers (people similar to yourself), and is therefore called **peer pressure**.

Compliance and internalisation

There is more than one way of reacting to pressure to conform. One reaction is **compliance** – when a person pretends to agree with the group while maintaining their own beliefs. Alternatively, the person might permanently adopt the behaviour, and continue to behave that way even away from group situations. This is known as **internalisation** (Kelman, 1958).

Top Tip

Distinguish between **compliance** and **internalisation** by asking yourself if a person would show a behaviour in private, or only in group situations.

Early research into conformity

Jenness (1932) conducted a study where individuals were shown beans in a jar and asked to **guess** their number. Participants were then put in groups and asked to **discuss** the number and give a **group estimate**. When later given the option of changing their first guess, most participants wanted to change to a number closer to the group estimate.

Sherif (1935) studied conformity using an illusion called the autokinetic effect, where a point of light appears to move in a darkened room. When alone, there was a wide variation in people's estimates of how far the light had travelled but if estimates were called out aloud in a group of three, a **group norm** emerged.

The length of lines study

In the early research into conformity, participants were asked questions that had **no clear right or wrong answer**. In contrast, Asch (1955) gave people a simple task. Participants were shown two cards – a standard card with one line on it and a comparison card with three lines. They were then asked which line from the comparison card was the same length as the line on the standard card. When alone, over 99% of participant responses were correct.

When participants were placed in a group of **stooges**, all of whom had been briefed to give the **wrong answer**, conformity emerged. There were 18 trials, and on 12 of these (the 'critical trials'), the stooges gave the same wrong answer as each other. The true participant was always last or second last to answer. Out of 123 participants on 12 critical trials, 37% of answers conformed to the majority.

Despite the fact that they **knew the correct answer**, participants were pressured into giving wrong answers – they showed **compliance**. 75% gave a wrong answer at least once. Asch interviewed participants afterwards, discovering that many gave the wrong answer to **avoid ridicule** from the majority.

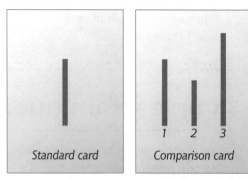

Standard card Comparison card

Asch used clear images of lines

Evaluation

- The Asch study lacks ecological validity: the task was artificial, and real-life situations are rarely so clear cut.
- Perrin and Spencer (1980) **replicated** the Asch study using engineering students, and found a much lower level of conformity than the original study.
- Moscovici (1981) believes that in the real world, compliance with a majority viewpoint rarely has any long-term impact on a person's behaviour.

Two types of social influence

The research into conformity shows two distinct types of social influence (Deutsch and Gerrard, 1955).

Top Tip

ISI tends to lead to internalisation, NSI tends to lead to compliance.

Informational social influence (ISI) is when uncertainty leads to a person adopting the behaviour of others; they conform because they want to be right. The studies by Sherif and Jenness demonstrated ISI. An example of ISI is a person copying others if they don't know what to do on an unfamiliar transport network.	
Normative social influence (NSI) is when a person is not in doubt, but is influenced by social norms. This is based on a need to be liked and accepted by others. NSI was a major factor in Asch's study. An example of NSI is when someone starts liking the same films and bands as their friends.	

Peer	Internalisation	ISI – informational social influence
Group pressure	Group norm	NSI – normative social influence
Compliance	Stooge	

Quick Test 30

1. Which type of social influence tends to result in compliance?
2. What percentage of Asch's participants conformed at least once?

Factors in conformity

What factors affect levels of conformity? What makes some people conform when others don't, or conform on some occasions and not others? The factors that affect conformity can be divided into two types: **situational factors** and **individual factors**.

Situational factors

Group size

Asch (1955) conducted several variations of his length of lines experiment, which showed the effect on conformity of being in a larger or smaller group. In each case, the level of conformity was different.

- With only one stooge, there was very little conformity.

- With two stooges, the conformity rate was just over 12%.

- With three stooges, the rate rose to over 30%.

- The addition of further stooges made only a **slight difference** to results.

What can be seen from these results is that the rise in total group size from three to four is critical. After that, adding an additional person (e.g. increasing group size from five to six) had little effect. However, the real world may be different to this artificial setting – in a lab, participants may suspect a trick if the confederates all give **the same wrong answer** (Baron and Byrne, 1997).

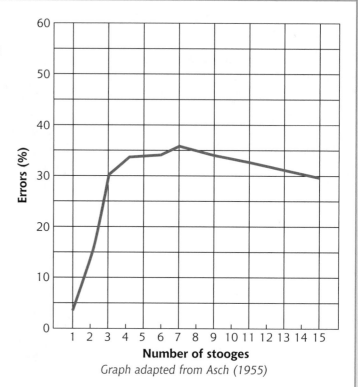

Graph adapted from Asch (1955)

An ally

Another variation of Asch's procedure was to provide an 'ally' by instructing one stooge to **disagree with the majority**, so that they were no longer unanimous. This decreased conformity, even when the stooge gave an answer more extremely wrong than the majority! When the majority were not **unanimous**, conformity stood at around 9%.

Similarity of the group

Experiments on conformity tend to use strangers but, away from the laboratory, we are most likely to be influenced by **people we know**, and who are like ourselves. Abrams et al. (1990) found that if participants feel that they share characteristics with the majority, they are more subject to **NSI** in an Asch-type situation.

Top Tip

Exam questions on factors in conformity tend to be poorly answered. Use the headings here as triggers for your answer, and include research evidence to help pick up A & E marks.

Individual factors

Gender

Some researchers have found **gender** differences in conformity, with women tending to conform more than men. Eagly (1987) has linked this to men trying to be independent and women trying to promote harmony in the group. However, the behaviour of males and females varies greatly over time, and depends on **culture**. Therefore such studies of gender differences in conformity may be culturally biased and outdated.

Culture

Smith and Bond (1993) analysed conformity studies from around the world, and found more conformity in **collectivist** societies (places where family and society are the highest priorities, for example most African and Asian countries) than in **individualist** societies (places where individual success is prioritised, for example USA and Western Europe). This could be because in collectivist societies, people try harder to achieve **group harmony**, resulting in conformity to the norm.

Personality

Burger (1992) has shown that people who value **personal control** are less likely to conform.

However, in the Stanford Prison Experiment, Zimbardo *et al.* (1973) did not support the idea that social behaviour comes from personality; they concluded that behaviour is mainly influenced by **social context**.

Top Tip

Think of real-life situations where conformity might be a problem, such as pressure to smoke cigarettes, and use this example in your essay. Sticking to one clear example will give coherence to your answer.

> Conformity   Unanimous   Personality   Gender   Culture

Quick Test 31

1. At what point did raising group size make the biggest difference to conformity?

Obedience

Obedience is a form of social pressure but, unlike conformity, which is unspoken, obedience is the response to a **direct order** or instruction. Pressure to conform tends to come from peers, but obedience is the result of an **authority figure** telling you what to do.

The Milgram study (1963)

The best-known study of obedience was conducted by Stanley Milgram in the early 1960s. Milgram wanted to explain why German soldiers and concentration camp guards had followed immoral orders during the Second World War, and aimed to find out if German people were naturally more obedient.

He conducted an experiment in New York (the original plan was to test German participants at a later date, but this never happened) using **fake electric shocks**. Forty participants believed they were giving shocks to a stooge who had been introduced as 'Mr Wallace'. They were told that they would play the role of **teacher** in an experiment about **memory** and learning, when in fact the aim was to study their **willingness to obey**. The electric shock apparatus had a series of switches, the first of which was labelled 15V with the voltage supposedly increasing by a further 15V with each subsequent switch; participants were asked to increase the shock level with each wrong answer. There were labels below the switches; for example, 375V – 'Danger, severe shock'. The last switch was labelled 450V.

Top Tip

Make sure your description of the procedure of Milgram (1963) is not overly long, and that the information you give is appropriate to the exam question!

A photograph from Milgram's obedience study

Procedure	The stooge made many mistakes, and at each one the participant had to press a higher-voltage switch. The stooge participant grunted with pain at first and, as the faked shocks continued, began to shout in protest, including saying that he had a heart condition, and refused to take any further part. After 315V he was silent. If the true participant hesitated, the researcher could use a verbal prod such as 'The experiment requires that you continue', or 'You have no choice, you *must* go on'.
Results	Prior to the study, Milgram's students and colleagues had thought that **American** participants would not obey the instructions. They predicted that just 3% of participants would continue right up to the 450V level. In fact, **65% obeyed**. Many showed signs of being stressed by the experiment, but none stopped before 300V.

Evaluation

This was the first major experimental study of obedience, and was particularly valuable in showing a truly unexpected result. The ethics of the study have been called into question, with participants suffering emotional harm. However, Milgram defended the study, stating that in a subsequent survey, 84% of participants said that they were 'glad to have been in the experiment', and that participants had been assessed by a psychiatrist, and had no signs of long-term harm (Colman, 1987).

Other studies of obedience

Subsequent research has found similar high levels of obedience in more realistic circumstances.

Hofling *et al.* (1966) conducted a field experiment with nurses. A fake drug was left in the ward, and nurses were instructed **over the telephone** to administer a dose of the drug which was much higher than the safe level indicated on the label. Despite having the opportunity to refuse, 21 out of 22 nurses prepared the medication and were going to administer it until stopped by the experimenter.

Sheridan and King (1972) conducted a replication of Milgram's procedure using real (though mild) electric shocks, and **puppies** as recipients of the shocks. Despite the obvious distress to the animals, 75% of participants obeyed instructions to the maximum level.

> Obedience   Direct order   Authority figure

Quick Test 32

1. How many participants took part in Milgram's (1963) study?

Factors in obedience

Why do people obey authority?

Milgram (1963) had not expected such high levels of obedience among Americans. His results clearly went against the initial 'Germans are different' hypothesis, instead suggesting that most people tend to obey authority.

Milgram had several ideas about why obedience levels were so high.

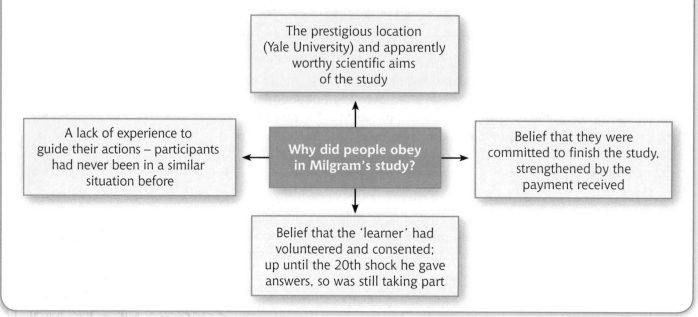

The prestigious location (Yale University) and apparently worthy scientific aims of the study

A lack of experience to guide their actions – participants had never been in a similar situation before

Why did people obey in Milgram's study?

Belief that they were committed to finish the study, strengthened by the payment received

Belief that the 'learner' had volunteered and consented; up until the 20th shock he gave answers, so was still taking part

Authority figures and socialisation

The level to which the authority figure seems to have **the right to give orders** is called the **perceived legitimate authority**. In society, some people are assumed to have this right. In one study, a person gave orders to passers-by (such as 'pick up that litter') while dressed in various outfits – security guard, milkman's uniform or casual clothes (Bickman, 1974). Being dressed as a security guard led to the greatest obedience – they are seen as authority figures. In Milgram's study, the experimenter, viewed as a scientist in charge of important research, was perceived to have legitimate authority.

Our tendency to obey authority figures is the product of **socialisation**. We are brought up from a young age to obey those in authority, which in childhood includes our parents and teachers.

Factors in obedience

To investigate the factors which affect obedience, Milgram (1974) performed several variations on the basic procedure.

Close proximity	Teacher sitting in same room as Mr Wallace, so could see as well as hear him. Obedience rate: 40%
Touch proximity	Teacher had to hold Mr Wallace's arms down, believing that shocks were delivered through metal plates on the chair arms. Obedience rate: 30%
Remote authority	Authority figure gave initial instructions and then left the room. Further instructions delivered by phone. Obedience rate: 20·5%
Peers rebel	Teacher paired with two stooge teachers who had been instructed to rebel at specific points (150V and 210V). Obedience rate: 10%
Peer gives shock	Teacher paired with another stooge teacher, whose job it was to press the shock switches. Obedience rate: 92·5%

In the standard procedure, having a wall between the participant and Mr Wallace acts as a **buffer**, making it easier to deliver the shock. The effects of **proximity** showed that while the immediate presence of Mr Wallace discouraged some participants, the compulsion to obey the authority figure was still very strong. However, when the authority figure was no longer present in the room, obedience fell sharply.

Perhaps the biggest effect was the use of **peers**. If another person **took responsibility** by pressing the switch, a much higher proportion of participants continued to the maximum shock level. If peers **rebelled**, the participant was much more likely to stop.

Agentic vs autonomous state

Milgram believed that we have two states of behaviour. In the **autonomous** state, we feel that we have control. This means that we take responsibility for our own actions.

The **agentic** state means that we think we are an agent carrying out someone else's wishes. In an authority situation, we cease to act autonomously. Because we allow another person to take charge, our moral values are not applied. In Milgram's (1963) study, people may have acted immorally because they accepted that the researcher took overall responsibility.

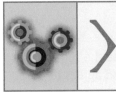

Perceived legitimate authority	Peer	Socialisation
Proximity	Autonomous	Agentic
Buffer		

Quick Test 33

1. Which variation of Milgram's basic procedure produced the lowest level of obedience and which produced the highest?

Resisting social pressure

There are several **strategies** that can be used to resist social pressure.

- Moral reasoning and awareness of own values
- Disobedient models
- Questioning motives of others including advertisers and peer groups

Moral reasoning and awareness of own values

The theory

Kohlberg (1969) believed that moral development proceeds in stages throughout life. Some people never achieve the highest stage of moral development, **post-conventional reasoning**, which involves an understanding that society's rules and conventions are not always morally right. An awareness of one's own values, and confidence in these values, can help people to resist conformity.

Research

Hornsey *et al.* (2003) found that if someone has a **strongly held conviction** about an issue, they are less likely to conform. In a follow up to Asch's study, Perrin and Spencer (1980) found that engineering students were much less likely to conform. This may relate to their self-confidence in their own ability to make visual judgements. Confidence is promoted in schools, and may help young people resist the pressure to abuse alcohol and drugs.

Evaluation

This theory helps to explain why some people act immorally, but raising people's moral development is very difficult. It is not practical as a short-term strategy.

Questioning motives

The theory

Another factor affecting compliance is the ability to question motives.

To achieve sales, certain **compliance techniques** are sometimes used.

Door-in-face technique	A high, unreasonable demand, followed by the lower (real) demand. Because the seller appears to have compromised, the customer feels pressured to do so too, and agrees to the lower demand.
Foot-in-the-door technique	A small trivial 'favour' is asked. Having agreed once, customers are much more likely to agree to a bigger demand than if that demand had been made straight away (Freedman and Fraser, 1966).
Low-ball technique	A low cost offer is made, and with agreement already achieved, extra costs are later added. Having already accepted, the customer feels they cannot pull out.

The low-ball is similar to Milgram's obedience study – participants had agreed to take part, and didn't feel they could pull out when greater 'costs' (in terms of stress) were later revealed.

Cults are experts in using compliance techniques, making people feel that they have made a commitment that they cannot escape from. **Raising awareness** of these techniques makes them much less powerful.

Evaluation

Simply making people aware of the techniques that are used can help people to resist them.

Anderson and Zimbardo (1984) state that it is important that people avoid making decisions when under stress, and avoid making decisions when in the presence of the person who triggers the stress.

The foot-in-the-door technique is used to achieve sales (Freedman and Fraser, 1996)

Disobedient models

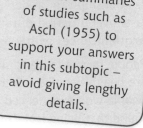

The theory

As Milgram (1974) demonstrated, having peers who refused to continue led to the lowest levels of obedience. In Asch's study, the presence of just one other group member who disagreed with the majority was enough to reduce conformity to under 10%. Both of these studies show the potential effect on our behaviour if other people in society resist social pressure. These disobedient peers act as **role models**, making it easier for others to do the same.

Top Tip

Use brief summaries of studies such as Asch (1955) to support your answers in this subtopic – avoid giving lengthy details.

Research

In a partial replication of Hofling *et al.*'s (1966) study of obedience, Rank and Jacobson (1977) found that only 11% of nurses obeyed when they were allowed to check with a colleague. The idea that disobedience is more likely when people are allowed to discuss their course of action was supported by Gamson *et al.* (1982), who found greater levels of dissent when people were put into groups, and allowed to mix and discuss their ideas.

Top Tip

Think about how these three strategies can be combined into a 20-mark essay answer. This can be drafted out in advance of the exam.

Evaluation

Experimental evidence supports the strong effect of disobedient models on our behaviour. Children could be encouraged to discuss a problem with friends or guidance staff at school, for example, when they are being pressured into doing something. Telephone helplines may also be valuable.

A limitation is that all too often in the real world, there is no disobedient model to help people resist obedience.

Some real-world evidence goes against the value of disobedient models. During the Second World War, the Nazi soldiers of Reserve Police Battalion 101 murdered Jewish civilians despite being given the option to be assigned to other duties. Despite several 'disobedient models', 80% of the troops continued to carry out the killings (Browning, 1992).

Sample exam questions

1. Why do people conform? Include research evidence in your answer. (12, 8)
2. Discuss the factors that affect obedience, referring to research evidence. (12, 8)
3. Discuss strategies that can be used to resist social pressure or coercion, referring to relevant research evidence. (12, 8)

Quick Test 34

1. Name three strategies for reducing social pressure.
2. Which study showed that people with strong values are less likely to conform?

The nature of affiliation and attraction

Affiliation

Affiliation means the human tendency to seek the company of others. This can be done for various reasons, including **avoiding loneliness**, reducing anxiety through **emotional support**, or to gain **attention**.

Humans have a basic need to form **social relationships** of various kinds. A relationship can be defined as any contact a person has with another person which lasts over a period of time. This includes **romantic relationships**, **friendships** and **acquaintances** with work colleagues, neighbours, etc.

People have a lot to gain from social relationships. As well as **social support**, there are health benefits – Cutrona *et al.* (1986) found that stress levels were lower among people who experienced a lot of social interaction, while Holt-Lunstad *et al.* (2010) found that being **isolated** can be as much of a risk to health as smoking or alcohol consumption.

> ### Top Tip
> The term social relationship includes both romantic relationships and friendships. When talking about relationships in your essay, it must be clear which kind of relationship you mean.

Attraction

Interpersonal **attraction** refers to the various ways in which a person might **like** other people, often leading to a friendship or romantic relationship.

Attraction is a narrower term than affiliation – people may affiliate with others without necessarily being attracted to them. For example, someone may choose to spend time with work colleagues to help advance their career, yet find them unattractive. However, in most cases, some type of attraction will be the **starting point of a relationship**.

There are several factors which affect how attracted we are to other people, including how familiar they are, and how similar they are to ourselves.

Similarity

Similarity means how alike people are. If the popular notion that 'opposites attract' is true, then similarity should count against relationships being formed. However, similarity has a positive effect on social relationships of all kinds, with relationships more likely to form and be maintained if people are similar.

Areas of similarity could include values, personality, ethnicity, employment, political stance and interests. Rubin (1973) suggests that similarity may:

- facilitate communication
- make it easier to find shared activities
- reassure us that others approve of us

> Between the concept of similarity and the matching hypothesis in the following subtopic.

Familiarity

Familiarity means how well a person feels that they know another person. How often people have **encountered** each other has a profound effect on affiliation and attraction, with people more likely to be attracted to others who are familiar. There are individual differences – some enjoy **meeting new people** while others find it worrying, and would strongly prefer to maintain relationships with people whom they already know well.

Simply being in someone's company without interacting can improve how likable they seem (Saegert *et al.*, 1973). However, in the real world it can be unclear whether we like people because we spend more time with them, or vice versa.

Top Tip

You only need to study **one** out of the three social psychology topics – prejudice, social relationships or conformity and obedience.

Proximity

Going hand-in-hand with familiarity is **proximity** – how close people are in terms of their physical location. You are much more likely to form a relationship with someone if they are nearby and you see them often.

The effect of proximity is most radically demonstrated in **Stockholm syndrome** – the condition where hostages display an irrational attraction to their captors. This is named after a bank robbery in the city of Stockholm, Sweden, where four bank workers expressed concern and liking for the robbers who held them captive in a bank vault and made numerous threats to their lives.

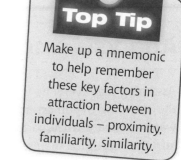

Top Tip

Make up a mnemonic to help remember these key factors in attraction between individuals – proximity, familiarity, similarity.

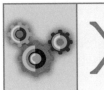

> Affiliation   Attraction   Familiarity
>
> Similarity   Proximity

Quick Test 35

1. Which is the broader term – attraction or affiliation?
2. Do opposites attract?

Attractiveness and relationship choice

Physical attractiveness

Particularly in Western societies, it is often assumed that **physical attractiveness** plays a key role in forming relationships. An early research study into this area used an artificial set-up called the **computer dance** (Walster *et al.*, 1966). 752 students filled in a questionnaire and were then allocated a partner for a date to a university dance, supposedly selected by a computer, but allocation was actually **random**. Physical attractiveness was found to be the most important factor in liking of partners, ahead of intelligence or personality.

However, later research found that when participants had a chance to meet beforehand (a more realistic scenario), partners who were **similar in physical attractiveness to each other** expressed the most liking.

The idea that couples choose partners who have a similar level of attractiveness to themselves is called the **matching hypothesis**. In a further study, real-life **engaged couples** were judged to be more similar to one another in attractiveness than randomly paired photographs (Murstein, 1972).

Analysis and evaluation

Assuming that everyone wants the most attractive partner possible, the concept of the matching hypothesis makes sense when it comes to partner choice – nobody wants an unattractive partner, but a person attempting to find a partner of higher attractiveness than themselves is more likely to experience failure/rejection.

A weakness of the Walster studies is that they were based on a short-term date, where participants had little to judge each other by except physical attractiveness. The studies also focused on **facial appearance** only, and ignored aspects such as body shape.

The matching hypothesis may not apply just to appearance – other factors such as wealth and education level may also be subject to matching (see previous section on similarity, above).

Top Tip

The matching hypothesis can be used to support answers on all areas of this topic.

Economic theories

One explanation of the matching hypothesis is that people avoid disappointment by aiming only as high as they can achieve. This is linked to **economic theories** of relationships, which state that relationships form through a series of **rational choices**.

Thibaut and Kelley (1959) suggested that a relationship involves many everyday **social exchanges** between partners, in which a partner can get a good or a bad deal.

Every individual will try to minimise their **costs**, and get as much **benefit** as possible out of the relationship. According to this view, a relationship will last if **both** partners are getting **more benefit than cost**.

Rewards	Costs
• Care • Childcare • Companionship • Fun • Sex • Increased reputation • Fidelity	• Effort • Time • Money • Wasted opportunities • Infidelity

A person **judges** the relationship they are in against a **comparison level** (CL) – a **schema** of what relationships should be like based on their past experiences as well as their views of what relationships ought to be like.

According to this model, a relationship will progress through up to four stages:

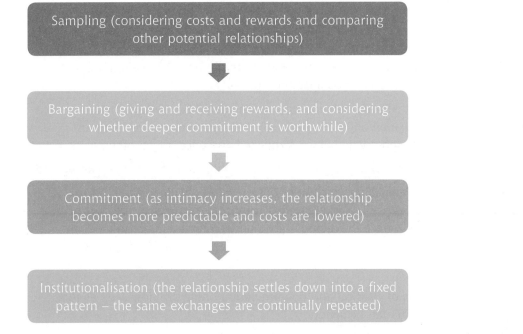

Sampling (considering costs and rewards and comparing other potential relationships)

Bargaining (giving and receiving rewards, and considering whether deeper commitment is worthwhile)

Commitment (as intimacy increases, the relationship becomes more predictable and costs are lowered)

Institutionalisation (the relationship settles down into a fixed pattern – the same exchanges are continually repeated)

(Based on Thibaut and Kelley, 1959)

Evaluation

This theory helps explain why so many people stay in bad or abusive relationships (investment is high and alternatives are unattractive), but Miller (2005) states that it is unrealistic to **reduce** human relationships to a series of rational choices. The theory is based on maximum reward to the self, but Walster *et al.* (1978) suggest that relationships which lack a **balance of rewards** between the partners are liable to break down.

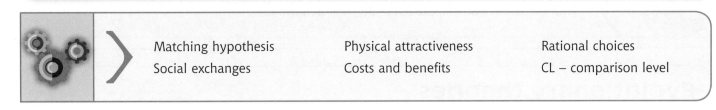

Matching hypothesis   Physical attractiveness   Rational choices
Social exchanges   Costs and benefits   CL – comparison level

Quick Test 36

1. What are the four stages in the economic theory of relationships?

Theories of attraction

The previous section explained how **economic theories** see relationships as a series of rational choices. The following sections explain two other major theories about how relationships are formed and maintained.

Learning theory

Learning theory states that our behaviour is based on **classical and operant conditioning**. The **behaviourist approach** sees relationships as a set of behaviours, subject to modification through learning by association, and through reward and punishment.

Top Tip

Relationship breakdown is no longer part of the Higher course.

Once a behaviour has been established, according to this view, it will be maintained by **reinforcement**. This means the repeated rewards that a person gets from being in the relationship, such as fun and companionship.

There is some evidence that social relationships are mediated by reinforcement. Jennings (1950) found that among 400 girls in a youth detention centre, the most popular individuals were those who helped, protected and encouraged others.

Some relationships are more rewarding than others, or they may start out rewarding and become unpleasant.

Extinction means that behaviours which were once rewarded will eventually stop if the rewards stop. Behaviourists would argue that **romantic gestures** at the start of a relationship are similar – once the relationship is underway, the romance tends to dwindle.

Evaluation

- Behaviourist concepts of classical and operant conditioning are now seen as too simplistic to explain human behaviour.

- The theory is very **individualistic**, and fails to explain behaviour in **collectivist cultures**, where relationships are strongly influenced by a person's family or community.

- Hill (1970) showed that family bonds are very resilient, and do not depend on short-term reinforcement.

> With the behaviourist approach in atypical behaviour.

Evolutionary theories

Evolutionary theories of relationships (also called **sociobiological** theories) are based on Darwin's theory of **evolution by natural selection**. Natural selection, as it is applied to psychology, means that people (or animals) will try to engage in behaviour which increases their **reproductive success**. This can mean producing a lot of offspring, or having fewer offspring and caring for them well.

Females put in more **reproductive investment**, with nine months of pregnancy followed by breastfeeding and (usually) having to do most of the childcare. Women can have relatively few children during their lives; males could potentially have a large number of children with many women.

What this means in terms of relationships is that for **women** the best evolutionary strategy is to look after their children well and seek a partner who is willing to provide support. If **men** enter into a long-term relationship, they will want to ensure that the woman is **fertile** and stays **faithful** (so that the children have his genes).

This results in the prediction that men will seek youthful women who can potentially have a lot of healthy offspring, and women will seek high-status men who can protect them and their children. Buss (1989) supported this idea: in a study of 37 different countries, women were found to prefer older men, and men to prefer younger women.

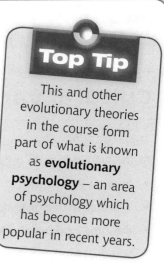

Top Tip

This and other evolutionary theories in the course form part of what is known as **evolutionary psychology** – an area of psychology which has become more popular in recent years.

Evaluation

- Based on the well-established theory of evolution by natural selection.

- Cannot explain same-sex relationships, or other relationships where reproduction is impossible.

- A limitation is the **cultural variation** in what is found to be attractive. Sometimes what is seen as attractive within a culture is *not* beneficial to reproduction, for example extreme thinness.

- Does not take into account conscious thought processes, for example thinking about the consequences of a relationship.

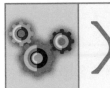

Classical conditioning	Operant conditioning	Extinction
Reinforcement	Natural selection	Evolutionary psychology
Reproductive investment		

Quick Test 37

1. Why do behaviours suffer from extinction?
2. Give one example of how males and females may have different evolutionary strategies.

Relationship variations

Cultural variation

There are differences between cultures, from the first interpersonal contact through to the way long-term relationships are managed. Cultural differences include:

- level of eye contact

- whether males or females (or both) tend to initiate relationships

- the type of dating/courting which takes place

Goodwin (1999) reported that there are cultural differences in the type of **love** that tends to occur. In American students, **companionate love** (focus on a loving affection and friendship) was most common, while Hispanic students were found to be high in **passionate/romantic love** (intense, unrealistic and emotional).

Within any culture or nation there are many **subcultures** – groups which have their own specific cultural values (e.g. punks). Subcultures tend to have their own styles of relationship, as well as variations in how relationships are formed.

> **Top Tip**
>
> It is likely that an exam essay question will allow you to write about more than one type of relationship variation.

Mediated relationships

A mediated relationship is one which forms **indirectly**, rather than through attraction when meeting face-to-face.

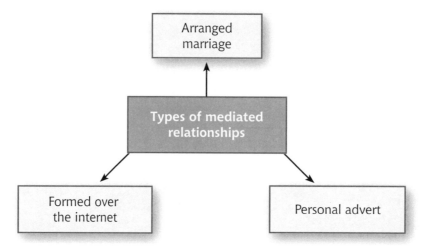

The **internet** is an increasingly popular way for relationships to be formed and maintained. Relationships may form through **social networking sites**, such as Facebook, and **discussion forum** websites. Sometimes, two people who form an online friendship never actually meet in person.

A personal advert is a notice in a newspaper or magazine placed by someone looking to meet someone new, usually for a romantic date. Romantic relationships are also formed online: **internet dating** is becoming increasingly common, with over five million people in the UK signed up to internet dating sites. A recent study found that despite the ease of video-chat online, most people preferred text-only contact in the early stages of a relationship (Gavin *et al.*, 2007).

Daredevil F seeks adventure sports-loving M for skiing, paragliding and abseiling fun. Must be up for anything!

- Genuine Guy, likes reading and cooking, seeks fun-loving F 20–40 year old for good times and fun chat

- Austrian psychotherapist, male, seeks patient with unresolved childhood conflicts for good-natured, one-sided conversation and possibly more...

- Shy and retiring F seeks com for quiet weekend trainspo interested, contact me via – www.ilovetrains.co.uk

Evaluation

There may be concerns about overusing the internet instead of having real-world interactions, but for many people the internet provides a non-threatening alternative to real-world networking, increasing their chances of forming meaningful relationships (Campbell *et al.*, 2006).

Individual variation

People conduct personal relationships in various ways, and Hazan and Shaver (1987) found that these appear to follow a similar pattern to childhood **attachments** – secure, insecure (avoidant) and insecure (resistant). While **secure** individuals can accept a variation in closeness with the partner, **resistant** individuals are anxious, jealous and need a lot of reassurance, and **avoidant** adults tend to keep others at a distance and avoid closeness.

Some relationships are harmful or abusive. Forward (1997) describes the process of **emotional blackmail**, where a person uses fear, obligation and guilt to manipulate their partner.

There are **personality** differences in the way people conduct internet relationships. Tosun and Lajunen (2010) found that students high in **extraversion** (being outgoing and talkative) tended to use the internet to **extend real-life relationships**, whereas students who scored high on **psychoticism** (being moody and aggressive) tended to use it as a **substitute for face-to-face relationships**, finding it easier to reveal their true selves online.

Same-sex relationships

In many ways, homosexual romantic relationships are no different from heterosexual romantic relationships. However, being openly homosexual can lead to prejudice or worse, so homosexual relationships are sometimes kept secret from family and friends, particularly among young gay people.

Starting with Denmark in 1989, laws in many countries have been changed to allow marriage or **civil partnerships** (a legal equivalent to marriage) between gay couples. However, some other countries still threaten imprisonment or even the death penalty for homosexuality.

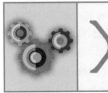

| Individual differences | Emotional blackmail | Cross-cultural differences |
| Same-sex relationships | Mediated relationships | |

Sample exam questions

1. With reference to research, discuss the nature of affiliation and attraction in social relationships. (12, 8)
2. Discuss individual and cultural variations in contemporary relationships. Refer to research evidence in your answer. (12, 8)

Quick Test 38

1. Give two examples of mediated relationships.

Definitions

If a behaviour is **atypical** it means that it is unusual in some way, and may be a sign of a psychological disorder. This is sometimes called **abnormal behaviour**, but the term **atypical behaviour** is preferred as it is less likely to cause offence.

Main definitions of atypical behaviour

Statistical infrequency

One way of defining atypical (or abnormal) behaviour is to say that it includes anything that occurs **infrequently**. Many psychological characteristics fall on a **bell-shaped curve** known as the **normal distribution**. The bulk of scores are close to the mean, and extreme values are rare. In intelligence, for example, it is rare to be extremely intelligent or extremely unintelligent, as most people would score between 70 and 130 on an IQ test.

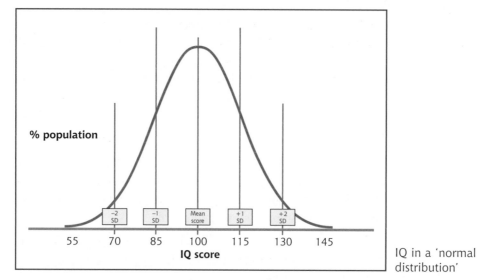

IQ in a 'normal distribution'

Advantages	Disadvantages
• This definition is objective – it does not rely on social norms or the opinion of a psychologist. • It fits what is usually understood by the word 'atypical', i.e. unusual.	• This definition is too broad: people with an IQ of 130+ are just as rare as those with an IQ of 70 and below, but don't usually need psychological help. • A person may be at the extreme end of a scale, such as the personality trait introversion, and yet live a happy and fulfilled life. Statistical infrequency can only be **part** of a complete definition of atypical behaviour.

Deviating from social norms

In this view, behaviour is atypical because it goes against the norms of society, and people therefore find it 'weird'. A **social norm** is an unwritten rule about what is right or wrong in social behaviour. Norms depend heavily on culture, varying between countries and over time.

Advantages	Disadvantages
• Fits with everyday experience of what people see as atypical.	• Every culture or subculture will have a separate viewpoint, so no worldwide standard of mental illness can be established using this definition. • Highly subjective. Too much reliance on one cultural view of right and wrong could lead to **discrimination**.

Distress

This definition is based on how a patient is feeling, and states that it is atypical to feel anxious, stressed or unhappy. Examples of psychological disorders which most obviously feature distress are **depression** and **anxiety disorders** (such as phobias).

Advantages	Disadvantages
• This is the basis on which someone is likely to seek help – they are suffering. • It is a practical definition in that it allows efforts to focus on helping the individual.	• Distress is not always the most important aspect of a disorder; in depression, other symptoms such as sleeplessness and loss of motivation are also important. • Some disorders lack this aspect completely. For example, a person with antisocial personality disorder feels no guilt and tends not to feel distress, but may be a danger to others.

Maladaptive behaviour

Maladaptive means something which harms an organism, i.e. reduces their chances of survival, or, more broadly, which harms an individual's ability to lead a fulfilled life. When diagnosing a disorder, a clinical psychologist will make an assessment of a patient's level of **functioning** – how they cope in everyday life, including maintaining relationships or holding down a job. Functioning is rated from 100 (the best) down to 0.

Top Tip

Include one or two briefly summarised research examples from later in this topic to back up your answer.

Advantages	Disadvantages
• A reasonably objective way of determining whether behaviours are causing a problem.	• Behaviours such as extreme sports may be dangerous but cause little or no harm to others, and people have a right to do them.

Top Tip

In an essay answer on definitions, you should include most or all of these different definitions. Look at each one as a building block for your answer.

| Atypical | Statistical infrequency | Social norms |
| Distress | Maladaptive | Functioning |

Quick Test 39

1. Which definition is based on how common a behaviour is?
2. What are social norms?

The medical model

What is the medical model?

The **medical model** (or 'biomedical model') seeks to explain atypical behaviour using the concepts of conventional **medicine**. It has resulted in medical terminology being used in atypical behaviour (e.g. 'diagnosis'), and the widespread view that psychological disorders are essentially **illnesses**. It is also associated with medical treatment, from drugs to hospitalisation.

Theoretically, the medical model is closely related to the **biological approach**, which states that behaviour stems from processes within the brain and body. The model also looks for genetic explanations for atypical behaviour.

There is good evidence that disorders are linked to biological processes. **Neurotransmitters** are messenger chemicals which get released into the **synapse** between neurons (brain cells), and **depression** has been linked to low levels of the neurotransmitter **serotonin**. Numerous disorders are associated with genetic factors – for example, depression is more likely in individuals who have an identical twin with the disorder (*McGuffin et al.*, 1996).

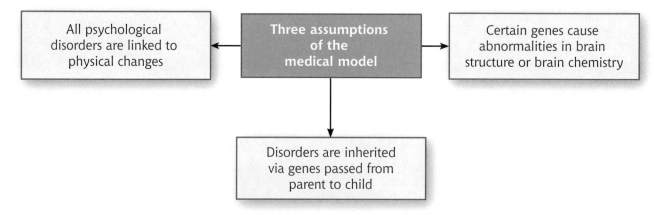

Evaluation

- Can be criticised for focusing on the symptoms of a disorder.
- Causes are assumed to be physical (in the brain/body), and the approach neglects psychological factors such as **beliefs**.
- The pharmaceutical industry has been criticised for promoting medication in the interests of profit.
- Brown and Harris (1978) found that working-class women were five times as likely to be depressed as middle-class women, suggesting that biological factors in depression could be of less importance than social factors, such as poverty.

To the topic of stress.

Medical therapies

Depression

Depressed patients tend to be prescribed **anti-depressant drugs** such as Prozac and Seroxat. These work by preventing the re-uptake of the neurotransmitter serotonin in the brain, making more of this chemical available. The benefits of these drugs support the medical view that serotonin plays a key role in depression.

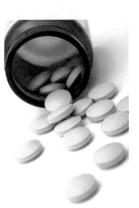

In extreme cases, where there is a suicide risk, **electroconvulsive therapy** (ECT) may be used. ECT is a method of inducing a seizure in an anaesthetised patient by applying a 70–150V **electric shock** to the head. This treatment is given two to three times a week for several weeks, and patients suffer from disorientation and may experience **memory loss**. It is controversial because, under the **Mental Health Act**, it can be administered without patients' consent if they are considered to be seriously ill and unable to make decisions for themselves.

Eating disorders

Patients with eating disorders can also benefit from anti-depressant drugs, or drugs which reduce anxiety. These drugs help patients come to terms with the underlying anxieties and insecurities which have made them vulnerable to the disorder.

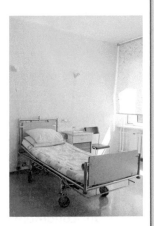

For anorexic patients with very severe weight loss, the emphasis is on **weight restoration** because of the great risks to their health. Again, in extreme cases, such as when an anorexic patient is viewed to be in danger of death, they can be forcibly hospitalised under the Mental Health Act.

Evaluation

- Medication is quick and easy to use, and usually cost-free to the patient. It provides relief, but does not tackle a patient's social problems. Drugs tend to have negative side effects.

- ECT can cause memory loss. Ng *et al.* (2000) found it to be effective, and stated that memories recovered within one month, but Youssef and Youssef (1999) claim that it is less effective than drug therapy, and should be abandoned altogether.

Top Tip

Medical therapies are easier to relate to depression; if you are focusing on eating disorders it is especially important to write a practice answer.

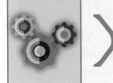

Biological approach	Hospitalisation	Neurotransmitters
Anti-depressant drugs	ECT – electroconvulsive therapy	Weight restoration

Quick Test 40

1. Which disorder(s) can be treated with anti-depressants?
2. What are the main side effects of ECT?

The cognitive and behaviourist approaches

The behaviourist approach

The **behaviourist approach** is based on two theories of learning – classical and operant conditioning. **Classical conditioning** states that two stimuli can be **associated** together, like **Pavlov's dogs** learning to associate food with a bell. Watson and Rayner (1920) used classical conditioning to teach a fear – while an infant was holding a white rat, a loud noise was made by banging an iron bar with a hammer. The child, 'Little Albert', soon showed an aversion to the rat!

Operant conditioning means learning on the basis of the outcome of an action. If actions have a bad outcome, an individual is less likely to repeat the action. Bandura *et al.* (1963) showed that operant conditioning can occur through observation of others' actions too. This is called **observational learning**, and could affect the development of atypical behaviour. For example, a vulnerable adolescent girl may see other girls being praised for their thin body shape. This would have a similar effect to her being directly rewarded for slimming.

Evaluation

- The behaviourist approach is simple and the theories are framed in a **testable** way, allowing for scientific research to take place.

- The approach cannot account for all aspects of human behaviour – by choosing to focus only on behaviours that can be observed from the outside, **thoughts and beliefs** are ignored.

The cognitive approach

The **cognitive approach** looks not just at what happens to the person and how they react, but also at the **mediating processes** in between, such as thoughts and beliefs.

Beck (1976) described how **cognitive errors** can have emotional and behavioural consequences. For example, **over-generalisation** means taking one event (such as falling out with a friend) and assuming it applies to all situations ('nobody likes me'). An anorexic person's cognitive error is the belief that they are overweight, which then leads to excessive dieting.

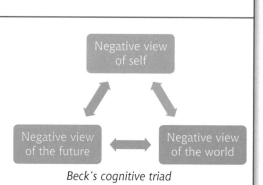

Beck's cognitive triad

Beck (1976) stated that depressed people have a **cognitive triad** of negative thoughts about themselves, the world and the future. These beliefs must be tackled in order to change a person's mood or behaviour.

Evaluation

- The cognitive approach is hugely influential, and its models of thought processes have influenced therapy and treatment methods.

- The approach is supported by research findings which show that thought processes are not always logical.

- Negative thoughts may sometimes be the **result** rather than the cause of conditions such as stress and depression (Schachter and Singer, 1962).

Cognitive-behavioural therapy (CBT)

Cognitive-behavioural therapy (CBT) draws on both of the above approaches. It aims to tackle cognitive errors – the therapist will ask questions, and **challenge** beliefs which seem irrational. The aim is to find more helpful ways of thinking and responding, in a process called **cognitive restructuring**.

Patients typically attend sessions once per week for between 5 and 20 weeks. There are also **behavioural tasks** which the patient should do between sessions, such as trying out new ways of reacting to situations.

Top Tip

Studies which compare different therapy choices make excellent evaluation points in your essays – and relate to more than one approach.

Depression

CBT attempts to tackle the cognitive triad of negative thoughts in depressed people. It works well, especially when combined with anti-depressant drugs. (APA, 2000)

Eating disorders

Cognitive distortions and negative attitudes and behaviours regarding food can be tackled using CBT. It is widely used for bulimia, with improvements in around 50% of cases. (Wilson, 1996)

Evaluation

- Widely used and respected – the most widely used psychological treatment on the NHS besides drugs.

- Less useful with anorexic patients whose attention span is affected by their severe weight loss, meaning that they struggle to concentrate during sessions.

- Elliott and Freire (2008) compared CBT to **humanist therapy** (see page 90). They stated that it was only slightly more effective, and that this small advantage could be due to therapists being biased in its favour.

From the topic of stress; **stress inoculation therapy** is a form of CBT.

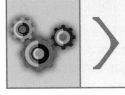

Behaviourist approach   Classical and operant conditioning   Cognitive approach
Mediating processes   Cognitive errors   Cognitive triad
CBT – cognitive-behavioural therapy

Quick Test 41

1. What type of conditioning was shown by Little Albert?

2. What is over-generalisation?

The psychoanalytic approach and therapy

The psychoanalytic approach believes that many psychological disorders in adults have their **roots in childhood**. Sometimes childhood memories are thought to have been **repressed** – pushed into the **unconscious** part of the mind, the **id** – because they are too painful or disturbing. A child's relationship with its parents is also seen as having a significant effect on behaviour.

Psychoanalysts view atypical behaviour as being a result of unconscious **conflicts** – behaviour may have a cause which is hidden in the unconscious. In Freud's study of 'Little Hans', a five-year-old boy suffered from a **phobia** of horses, Freud (1909) concluded that the boy's true problem was an unconscious fear of his father.

Depression

Psychoanalysis sees depression as having its roots in childhood. Freud believed that if a child is not loved and supported, anger towards the parents may become directed towards the self in the form of self-hatred. Repression of unpleasant memories also plays a role. Klein's (1957) view was that babies go through the **depressive position** (see section in 'Historical views of attachment', page 7), which, if not resolved, can lead to a tendency towards depression later in life.

Eating disorders

A controversial psychoanalytic explanation of anorexia was put forward by Hilde Bruch (1979), suggesting that it is based on a girl's repressed sexual desire. The adolescent girl **fears** sexual maturity, and unconsciously associates gaining weight with pregnancy. She then tries to lose weight in order to maintain a childlike state.

Supporting evidence comes from Freud's patient **Anna O**, who suffered from nausea (feeling sick) and had difficulty drinking. Freud and his colleague Breuer believed that her fear of drinking stemmed from a repressed memory of a dog drinking from her water glass. Freud claimed that when the memory was made conscious through therapy, the problem was solved (Freud, 1910). However, later researchers suggested that Anna suffered from epileptic seizures and drug dependence, making it impossible to generalise the findings of her case to the population as a whole.

Psychoanalytic therapy

Psychoanalytic therapy is still widely used today. It attempts to uncover and deal with the unconscious forces from the id and conflicts in development which affect a person's behaviour. As in the case of Anna O, the therapist will attempt to uncover repressed memories. A therapy session may involve a patient lying on a couch speaking, while the therapist listens, takes notes, and asks occasional questions.

There are three main techniques.

Dream analysis	Looking at symbols in dreams to reveal ideas in the unconscious mind. Freud believed the symbols in dreams are transformed to make them less shocking, but can reveal what we secretly desire.
Hypnosis	Putting a person into a relaxed, suggestible state so that they will reveal unconscious thoughts. However, not everyone can be easily hypnotised, and Freud came to regard the technique as unreliable.
Free association	Saying whatever comes to mind, and letting one idea lead to another in a continuous flow. Inspired by the case of Anna O, who would utter mysterious strings of words, this came to be the main technique of psychoanalytic therapy. It aims to access unconscious thoughts and memories.

A modern variant on psychoanalytic therapy is called **interpersonal therapy (IPT)**, and focuses on resolving family conflicts. This is particularly appropriate for teenagers, who may find it hard to adjust to their changing relationship with their family as they grow up.

Evaluation

- Freud's theories of the mind are controversial and there is a lack of research evidence to support them. Most psychoanalytic theories are **not testable**, and can therefore be considered unscientific.

- Dream analysis is one of Freud's most influential contributions to psychology, but it is impossible to verify whether interpretations of dreams are accurate.

- Shapiro *et al*. (1994) found IPT to be just as effective for depression as CBT.

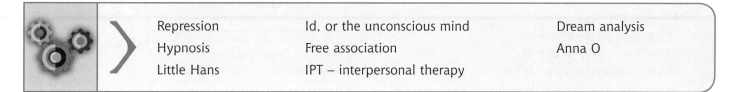

Repression	Id, or the unconscious mind	Dream analysis
Hypnosis	Free association	Anna O
Little Hans	IPT – interpersonal therapy	

Quick Test 42

1. Which of Freud's patients experienced nausea?
2. What is the main technique used in psychoanalytic therapy?

The humanist approach and therapy

Top Tip

For the exam, you only need to learn about the humanist approach **or** the psychoanalytic approach, not both.

While the psychoanalytic and behaviourist approaches see humans as slaves to the unconscious or to conditioning, the humanist approach, founded by Carl Rogers and Abraham Maslow, aimed to take a more positive approach to human psychology and to atypical behaviour. It states that everyone is **unique** and responsible for their own psychological health.

Hierarchy of needs

The **hierarchy of needs** is a humanist theory which states that the more basic human needs need to be satisfied before higher-level ones can be. Abraham Maslow (1943) presented this in the form of a pyramid-shaped diagram.

- Things like a love of learning (cognitive needs) or appreciation of art (aesthetic needs) are seen as impossible to achieve unless the individual has first satisfied their safety, belonging and esteem needs. So, for example, a child is unlikely to care about learning if they are being rejected by their peers.

- At the top of the hierarchy is what Maslow saw as the pinnacle of human development – **self-actualisation**. Maslow believed that only a few people ever achieve this, and used Albert Einstein and Abraham Lincoln as examples of people who have. One reason for this

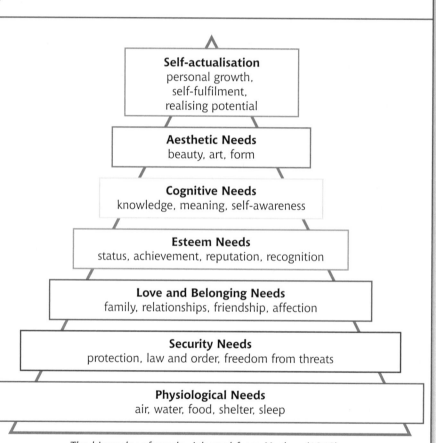

The hierarchy of needs. Adapted from Maslow (1943).

is the **Jonah Complex** – Maslow believed that, like the religious prophet Jonah who resisted God's call to go on an important mission, people fear their destiny and avoid striving for greatness (although, as an atheist, Maslow did not believe that destiny is set by God!).

> Between the humanist approach and Religious Studies. This movement tends to be associated with atheism, and you may have attended a humanist (non-religious) wedding ceremony.

Humanist therapy

On the surface, humanist therapy can resemble psychoanalysis – a discussion between an individual (usually referred to as a **client**) and a therapist, usually on a one-to-one basis. Humanist therapy is **client-centred**, which means that rather than being directed by the therapist, the client must make choices to resolve their problems.

Carl Rogers (1951) viewed therapy as a **relationship** between client and therapist, and stated that, for it to be successful, it must have three key elements.

Empathy	Attempting to perceive things as the client does; mentally taking their position to see why they are unhappy, anxious, etc.
Congruence	Being honest. Rogers maintained that, instead of being passive and pretending to know all the answers, therapists should show their feelings and admit to being unsure.
Unconditional positive regard	The therapist should be positive to the client and accept what they say, even if it seems strange.

Evaluation

- The humanist approach helped to challenge the negative view of human behaviour proposed by other approaches, and presented the benefits of positive thinking and taking control.

- It is still a major therapy choice but, as a general approach to psychology, its influence is small.

- Humanist therapy is individualistic, and the assumption that the client can work out problems on their own neglects the importance of **social relationships**.

- The therapy can be time-consuming and expensive but, in a review, Elliott and Freire (2008) found it to be just as effective as other major therapy choices.

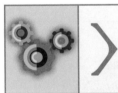

Hierarchy of needs	Self-actualisation	Client-centred therapy
Unconditional positive regard	Congruence	Empathy

Sample exam questions

1. Describe and evaluate **two** approaches to explaining psychological disorders. Refer to research evidence in your answer. (12, 8)

2. With reference to research, discuss the range of definitions of atypical behaviour. (12, 8)

3. Explain **two** therapy choices which could be used to treat depression or an eating disorder. (12, 8)

Quick Test 43

1. Name the humanist researcher who devised the hierarchy of needs.
2. What are the three elements of client-centred therapy?

Factor theories

The nature of intelligence and IQ

Top Tip

Start an exam essay with a clear definition of the term intelligence, including two or three aspects (see the first sentence in this section).

Intelligence is difficult to define but, broadly speaking, it is the ability or set of abilities which help us **think and reason** effectively, **take in information**, and **respond to the environment** effectively.

The first intelligence tests were developed by French psychologists Alfred Binet and Théodor Simon. They had been recruited by the French government to find an objective way of assessing which children needed extra help at school. A score on an intelligence test became known as **IQ** or **intelligence quotient**, and was calculated by dividing the child's mental age by their actual age in years, and multiplying the result by 100.

Curiously, the average IQ has increased year on year, at an average rate of around 3 points per decade (Flynn, 1984). This is known as the **Flynn effect**. Though not fully understood, it could be the result of better diet or improved **education**.

Top Tip

If relevant to the question, IQ can be defined as 'a numerical measure of intelligence using a test, where scores are placed on a scale with the average set at 100'.

The 'g' factor

Sir Charles Spearman was a psychologist who was also an expert in **statistics**. He found that schoolchildren's grades across seemingly unrelated subjects were positively correlated, and explained this pattern by referring to two factors – the **specific factor**, which varies depending on the type of task (e.g. spelling), and **g**, a **general factor** that is **constant** across all cognitive tasks (Spearman, 1904).

The concept of a single general factor underlying all intelligent behaviour is still known as **general intelligence**, or the **'g' factor**. Many researchers who believe in the 'g' factor also believe that it is largely **fixed**, and determined by **genetics**.

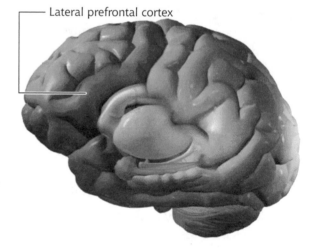

Lateral prefrontal cortex

A study by Duncan *et al.* (2000) suggested a possible brain area for the 'g' factor. Using brain scans, the researchers found that the **lateral prefrontal cortex** in the brain became active on the tests which required problem-solving, but not on similar tests with no problem-solving involved.

Evaluation of 'g'

The concept of 'g' relies on a statistical technique called **factor analysis**. Later statisticians came to different conclusions; Thurstone and Thurstone (1941) claimed that there was not one factor, but seven!

Robinson (2001) sees 'g' as a very narrow view of intelligence, which excludes practical, creative or emotional abilities.

Spearman's model lacks any clear explanation of how 'g' is supposed to function on a cognitive level. Nevertheless, the concept of 'g' is still widely accepted.

> **Top Tip**
>
> 'The **nature** of intelligence' is one part of the syllabus – don't get it mixed up with the **nature–nurture** debate (see page 96).

Fluid and crystallised intelligence

Cattell (1971) believed that 'g' should be subdivided into two types: **fluid intelligence** (Gf) and **crystallised intelligence** (Gc).

Fluid intelligence is seen to be the more **flexible** part of intelligence, and vital to solving **novel tasks**. It is genetically controlled and develops through childhood, but after reaching adulthood it is **fixed**.

Crystallised intelligence is the type of reasoning that is based on learned skills and **strategies,** which can develop separately for different types of tasks. As this can be learned from experience, crystallised intelligence **can increase** throughout life.

Evaluation of fluid and crystallised intelligence

- Cattell's model seems more realistic than the basic 'g' model as it explains why people can improve their performance on cognitive tasks later in life.
- It is still partly based on the controversial idea that intelligence is innate.

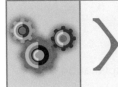

Intelligence quotient (IQ)	Flynn effect	'g' factor – general intelligence
Specific factor	Fluid intelligence	Crystallised intelligence

Quick Test 44

1. What statistical technique did Spearman use to develop his theory?
2. Which of the two types of intelligence in Cattell's model can develop throughout life?

Information processing approach

Modern theories of intelligence have moved away from the use of factor analysis because it analyses the results of tests without looking at the **processes** used to solve problems.

Information processing theories (also called **cognitive theories**) study the strategies a person uses as they solve problems. They are based on the analogy of the human mind to a computer, popular in the **cognitive approach**.

The triarchic theory

Robert Sternberg's **triarchic theory** of intelligence (Sternberg, 1988) aims to show that intelligence is not just about what happens in your head, but also how you react to **situations in the real world**. As the name 'triarchic' suggests, there are three parts to it, called 'subtheories'.

- **Analytic** (or 'componential') subtheory – the mental skills used for solving problems, including **reasoning**, **knowledge acquisition** and **metacognition** (i.e. analysis of our own thought processes).

- **Creative** (or 'experiential') subtheory – dealing with familiar or unfamiliar problems. This includes using creativity to deal with unfamiliar problems, and drawing on **experience** to solve familiar problems quickly.

- **Practical** (or 'contextual') subtheory – adapting to problems in the real world, rather than the abstract problems of an IQ test. People with high practical intelligence are very good at dealing with situations in the real world: they have 'street smarts'.

Top Tip

Your knowledge of each theory of intelligence is a building block for a longer exam answer. You should include at least two in an essay answer.

Evaluation

- Strengths of the theory include its explanation of creativity as part of intelligence, and the explanation of intelligence in context rather than just on abstract tasks.

- Unlike factor models, the different parts of this theory are explained in terms of cognitive processes.

Multiple intelligences

Another theory from the **information processing approach** is Howard Gardner's theory of **multiple intelligences**.

Gardner (1983) claims that there is no logical reason to call our linguistic and mathematical abilities 'intelligence', and not use the same term for things like our interpersonal or musical abilities. The theory sets out eight separate areas, all of which are termed 'intelligences'.

The key feature of this theory is that there are many intelligences, each of them totally **separate**. A person can be good or bad at any one. So, unlike the 'g' factor theory, being bad at maths does not mean you are stupid – you might have a low **logical-mathematic intelligence** but a high **musical** or **naturalistic** intelligence.

Unfortunately, most exams – including Higher Psychology – require a lot of writing, so people with high **linguistic** intelligence have an advantage. You can draw on your strengths in other areas in your revision – for example, using diagrams and mind maps if you are strong in **spatial** intelligence.

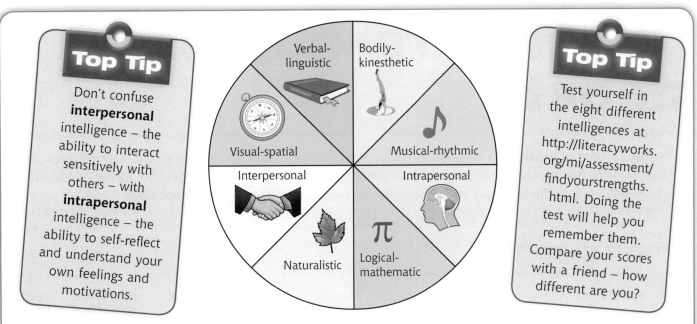

Top Tip

Don't confuse **interpersonal** intelligence – the ability to interact sensitively with others – with **intrapersonal** intelligence – the ability to self-reflect and understand your own feelings and motivations.

Top Tip

Test yourself in the eight different intelligences at http://literacyworks.org/mi/assessment/findyourstrengths.html. Doing the test will help you remember them. Compare your scores with a friend – how different are you?

Evaluation

- The theory has become popular among teachers, and has influenced educational practice to the benefit of students who aren't suited to traditional teaching methods.

- Gardner tends to support his ideas with case-studies, and the theory has been criticised for a lack of experimental research evidence (Sternberg and Grigorenko, 2004).

Summary

Theories of intelligence can be divided into two categories: factor models and information processing models:

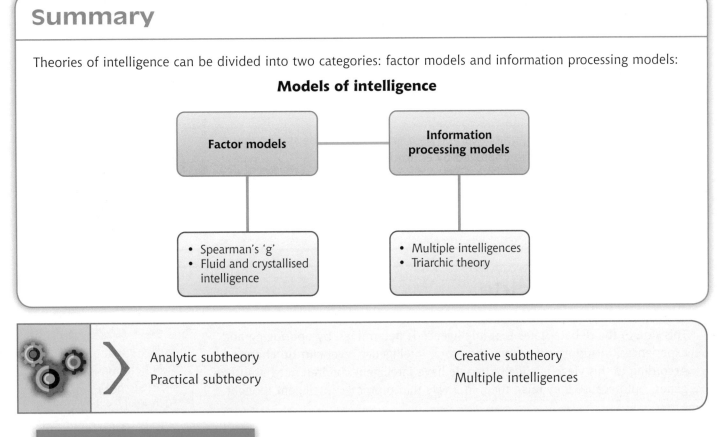

Models of intelligence

Factor models	Information processing models
• Spearman's 'g' • Fluid and crystallised intelligence	• Multiple intelligences • Triarchic theory

Analytic subtheory   Creative subtheory

Practical subtheory   Multiple intelligences

Quick Test 45

1. Which triarchic subtheory is relevant to using creativity?

2. Which of the multiple intelligences helps you understand your own feelings?

The nature–nurture debate

The nature–nurture debate is an ongoing discussion of the role of **nature**, i.e. genetic factors, and **nurture**, i.e. upbringing and experience, in psychology. It is an attempt to discover which of the two, nature or nurture, is most important in the development of characteristics such as **intelligence** and **personality**.

The nature side

The nature side of the debate states that intelligence is largely under **genetic control**, and we are therefore born to have a level of intelligence that cannot be significantly increased through experiences. This side states that a child's intelligence is **inherited** from their parents.

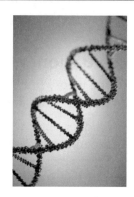

Research evidence

A **twin study** is a research study into **genetically identical twins**, who have been separated at a young age and raised in different environments. Bouchard and McGue (1981) found that over several such studies, the average **correlation** in IQ was 0·72, compared to just 0·24 for ordinary siblings reared apart (siblings share approximately 50% of the same genes).

Horn (1983) studied children who had been **adopted**, finding that they showed a 0·28 correlation with their natural mothers' IQ and a lesser 0·15 correlation with their adoptive mothers' IQ. However, both correlations are low, suggesting that experiences have a great impact on IQ.

Evaluation

• The nature side of the argument can be seen as pessimistic, by stating that IQ is innate and cannot be improved by education.

• The nature side has also been used to support a tenuous argument that intelligence depends on ethnicity.

The nurture side

This side of the debate states that intelligence is determined by upbringing and experiences, including education. Therefore, intelligence level **can be changed**. According to this view, intelligent people have intelligent children not because of genes, but because they **raise** them in a way that promotes intelligent thought.

Research evidence

Hart and Risley (1995) found evidence that positive **parenting** can increase verbal intelligence (a major part of IQ). Using tape recordings, they found wide variations in some aspects of parenting, such as using a wide **vocabulary** and asking their children questions. Children who heard more complex language

Top Tip

Use visual images to help remember researcher names such as 'Horn'. Active images work best – Skeels and Dye sounds rather like 'ski and die', forming an easy, gruesome image!

developed a broader vocabulary and scored higher in intelligence tests. This research benefited from using detailed observations and a longitudinal design.

> The nurture view also implies that children who are deprived of a stimulating environment will have a lower intelligence, and this has been shown in cases of **deprivation**. You can find more detail on studies of deprivation in the topic on 'Early Socialisation' (page 10).
>
> In addition, taking children out of an **institution** and putting them in an enriched environment can boost intelligence (Skeels and Dye, 1939). Animals also benefit from an **enriched environment**, and research on **rats** shows that their brains become more complex too (Kempermann *et al.*, 1997).
>
> Governments are aware that if children have less environmental stimulation at home it may harm their intelligence; in America, the **Head Start Program** is one initiative which provides improved education to children from impoverished families.

Interactionist approaches

Nowadays, many researchers have moved away from a simplistic 'either–or' debate and take an **interactionist** approach, meaning that both nature and nurture interact. For example, an individual might be born with a tendency to have a high level of intelligence, but due to negative life circumstances and experiences might not fulfil their potential. The way that genes behave can depend on the environment they are in. (Ridley, 2003)

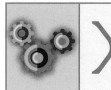

Nature	Nurture	Genetics	Twin study
Deprivation	Enriched environment	Interactionist	

Quick Test 46

1. What IQ correlation in identical twins did Bouchard and McGue (1981) report?
2. What is the term meaning that nature and nurture both play a role and affect each other?

Uses of IQ testing

IQ tests are the main way of assessing a person's intelligence. These tests typically have a mixture of **verbal**, **visual** and **logic-based** problem-solving questions. Results are converted into an IQ score.

Problems with IQ tests

It is difficult to write a good-quality IQ test. Some of the main challenges are as follows.

Cultural bias is where people from a particular culture have an advantage or disadvantage at a task.

Validity of any test is a term meaning how well it measures what it sets out to measure. The aim of any IQ test is to measure intelligence, but this is difficult as there are disagreements as to what intelligence is.

Reliability is the extent to which a test gets consistent results. Tests are carefully designed to increase reliability, but a person's IQ score can vary by as much as 15 points from one test to the next (Smith, 1991).

Top Tip

The reliability of a test is less valuable if the test does not measure what it aims to (i.e. if it lacks validity) – it can mean that a test is reliably misleading!

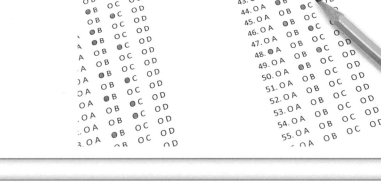

IQ testing in schools

IQ testing began in education with Binet and Simon's work in the French school system, and IQ tests continue to be widely used, for example as school **entry tests**. In Britain, the **11 plus test** was once used to allocate pupils to the type of secondary school they would attend, but this has now been abandoned.

Another use for IQ tests is **streaming** (also called 'tracking') – a system of dividing pupils into classes based on IQ or ability (rather than having **mixed ability** classes).

A **self-fulfilling prophecy** is when something becomes more likely because it has been predicted. Rosenthal and Jacobson (1968) found that streaming by IQ led to a self-fulfilling prophecy – in their study, children labelled as intelligent went on to increase in IQ. Teachers were given the names of certain pupils and told that they were going to do well over the year. The selected pupils went on to show the biggest **increases in IQ** – even though they had actually been selected at random! The study had the advantage of taking place in a real-world context. However, interfering in children's education in this way is **unethical**.

Streaming can improve education for the brightest pupils (Kulik and Kulik, 1992), but a major problem is that pupils in lower streams might feel inferior and lose motivation.

This issue often comes up in discussions of **politics** and educational policy.

IQ testing in the workplace

Intelligence tests are used by **employers** to help recruit staff.

It has been known for a long time that IQ tests are not always a good indication of how people will perform in practical situations (Wechsler, 1940). However, the tests are trusted because employers believe them to be more reliable than tests of other abilities such as interpersonal skills (Neisser *et al.*, 1996).

Experience of the job search process or your studies of Business Management will help here.

IQ testing in the army

One of the first workplaces to make use of IQ tests was the military.

During the First World War, psychologist Robert Yerkes tested 1·75 million army recruits and used the results to allocate men to army ranks. Yerkes also analysed IQ scores in terms of the men's nationality and ethnicity, and found that there were IQ differences between recruits of different ethnic origins.

However, Gould (1982) reviewed the procedures and findings, and spotted many flaws and biases. For example, not all of the recruits were literate or had a reasonable grasp of English. The results did not take into account **cultural bias** in the tests, which were more appropriate for middle-class whites. Education was a **confounding variable**, with many African American recruits having been educated only until age nine.

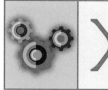

IQ – intelligence quotient	Reliability	Validity	Cultural bias
Entry test	Streaming	Recruitment	

Sample exam questions

1. Describe and evaluate two or more models of intelligence. (12, 8)
2. Discuss the nature-nurture debate, referring to research evidence. (12, 8)

Quick Test 47

1. Name two educational uses for IQ tests.
2. What was a weakness of the WW1 army IQ tests?

Answers to Quick Tests

Quick Test 1

1. Wanting to be near PAF, using them as base, orienting behaviour.

Quick Test 2

1. Operant conditioning.
2. The first stage of development in psychoanalytic theory.

Quick Test 3

1. Secure attachment.

Quick Test 4

1. Protest, despair, detachment.
2. Monotropy and critical period.

Quick Test 5

1. Privation
2. Koluchová (1991) or Curtiss (1977).

Quick Test 6

1. Social, cognitive and emotional development.
2. Variety of activities and child–staff ratio.

Quick Test 7

1. 7+/−2
2. Encoding, storage and retrieval.

Quick Test 8

1. The sensory memory.
2. Craik and Tulving (1975) and Morris *et al.* (1985).

Quick Test 9

1. The phonological loop.

Quick Test 10

1. Displacement
2. Proactive interference.

Quick Test 11

1. One had only three conditions, and asked the critical questions one week later.
2. Information after the event, social pressure, expectations, external appearance.

Quick Test 12

1. Any from: raised heart rate, sweating, tense muscles, increased blood clotting, heightened vision and awareness, glucose entering bloodstream, slowed digestion.
2. The autonomic nervous system and the endocrine system.

Quick Test 13

1. After 6–48 hours.

Quick Test 14

1. A person assesses their own ability to cope with stressors.

Quick Test 15

1. Males have a greater and more sustained release of adrenalin.

Quick Test 16

1. Anger and irritability/emotional outbursts/difficulty concentrating.

Quick Test 17

1. Conceptualisation, skills acquisition and application.
2. Underestimating the time it will take to do a task.

Quick Test 18

1. Independant measures and method participants.

Quick Test 19

1. A question with a fixed selection of answers.

Quick Test 20

1. Naturalistic
2. Lack of control OR hard to replicate.

Quick Test 21

1. Longitudinal, in-depth, individual case/small group.
2. Interviews, observations, brain scans, ability tests, etc.

Quick Test 22

1. There is no way of knowing which variable is affecting which; a third variable could be influencing both.
2. A straight line positioned to minimise distance between points and the line.

Quick Test 23

1. Random
2. Two

Quick Test 24

1. When there are extreme (high or low) scores.

Quick Test 25

1. No, parental consent is needed.
2. Yes, they can.

Quick Test 26

1. Cognitive, affective and behavioural.

Quick Test 27

1. Nine
2. Fascism

Quick Test 28

1. Social categorisation, social identification, social comparison and psychological distinctiveness.
2. Schoolboys

Quick Test 29

1. Self-esteem, liking for group members and academic performance.
2. Support from authorities, personal acquaintance, introduction to non-stereotypical individuals, cooperation between groups, and equal status.

Quick Test 30

1. Normative social influence.
2. 75%

Quick Test 31

1. The rise from three to four.

Quick Test 32

1. 40

Quick Test 33

1. Peers rebel; peer gives shock.

Quick Test 34

1. Moral reasoning, questioning motives, disobedient models.
2. Hornsey *et al.* (2003) or Perrin and Spencer (1980).

Quick Test 35

1. Affiliation
2. Rather than opposites, people tend to be attracted to those who are similar to themselves.

Quick Test 36

1. Sampling, bargaining, commitment, institutionalisation.

Quick Test 37

1. Because they are no longer rewarded.
2. Aim for different numbers of offspring OR males aim for youthful partner/females aim for partner who can support them.

Quick Test 38

1. Internet, arranged marriage or personal adverts.

Quick Test 39

1. Statistical infrequency.
2. Unspoken social rules.

Quick Test 40

1. Both depression and eating disorders.
2. Memory loss and disorientation.

Quick Test 41

1. Classical conditioning.
2. A distortion in thinking where one bad outcome is linked to many other situations.

Quick Test 42

1. Anna O
2. Free association

Quick Test 43

1. Abraham Maslow
2. Empathy, congruence, unconditional positive regard.

Quick Test 44

1. Factor analysis
2. Crystallised

Quick Test 45

1. Experiential
2. Intrapersonal

Quick Test 46

1. 0·72
2. Interactionist

Quick Test 47

1. Streaming, entry tests
2. Cultural bias

References

Abrams, D., Weherell, M., Cochrane, S., Hogg, M.A. and Turner, J.C. (1990). Knowing what to think by knowing who you are: self-categorisation and the nature of norm formation. *British Journal of Social Psychology, 29,* 97–119.

Adorno, T.W., Frenkel-Brunswik, E., Levinson, D.J. and Sanford, R.N. (1950). *The Authoritarian Personality.* New York: Harper.

Ainsworth, M.D.S. and Bell, S.M. (1970). Attachment, exploration and separation: illustrated by the behavior of two-year-olds in a strange situation. *Child Development, 41,* 49–65.

Allport, G. (1954). *The Nature of Prejudice.* New York: Double-Day Anchor.

Altemeyer, R. (1981). *Right-wing Authoritarianism.* Winnipeg: University of Manitoba Press.

Altemeyer, R. (2006). *The Authoritarians.* Retrieved 28 July 2010 from http://home.cc.umanitoba.ca/~altemey/

Anderson, S.M. and Zimbardo, P.G. (1984). On resisting social influence. *Cultic Studies Journal, 1* (2), 196–219.

APA (2000). *Practice Guideline for the Treatment of Patients with Major Depressive Disorder (2nd ed).* Washington, DC.: American Psychiatric Press Inc.

Aronson, E. and Bridgeman, D. (1979). Jigsaw groups and the desegregated classroom: in pursuit of common goals. In E. Aronson (ed.), *Readings About the Social Animal* (6th ed.). New York: W.H. Freeman.

Asch, S.E. (1951). Effects of group pressure upon the modification and distortion of judgment. In H. Guetzkow (ed.), *Groups, Leadership and Men.* Pittsburgh: Carnegie Press.

Asch, S.E. (1955). Opinions and social pressure. *Scientific American, 193,* 31–35.

Atkinson, R.C. and Shiffrin, R.M. (1968). Human memory: a proposed system and its control processes. In K.W. Spence and J.T. Spence (eds), *The Psychology of Learning and Motivation, Vol. 2.* London: Academic Press.

Baddeley, A.D. (1966). Short term memory for word sequences as a function of acoustic, semantic and formal similarity. *Quarterly Journal of Experimental Psychology, 18,* 362–65.

Baddeley, A.D. and Hitch, G. (1974). Working memory. In G.H. Bower (ed.), *The Psychology of Learning and Motivation, Vol. 8.* London: Academic Press.

Baddeley, A.D. and Hitch, G. (1977). Recency re-examined. In S. Dornic (ed.), *Attention & Performance.* New Jersey: Lawrence Erlbaum.

Baddeley, A.D., Grant, S., Wight, E. and Thomson, N. (1973). Imagery and visual working. In P.M.A. Rabbitt and S. Darnit (eds), *Attention and Performance V.* London: Academic Press.

Baddeley, A.D., Thomson, N. and Buchanan, M. (1975). Word length and the structure of short-term memory. *Journal of Verbal Learning and Verbal Behavior, 14,* 575–89.

Bandura, A., Ross, D. and Ross, S.A. (1963). Transmission of aggression through imitation of aggressive models. *Journal of Abnormal and Social Psychology, 66,* 3–11.

Baron, R.A. and Byrne, D. (1997). *Social Psychology* (8th ed.). London: Allyn & Bacon.

Bartlett, F.C. (1932). *Remembering.* Cambridge: Cambridge University Press.

Bass, B.M. (1955). Authoritarianism or acquiescence? *Journal of Abnormal and Social Psychology, 51,* 616–23.

Baydar, N. and Brooks-Gunn, J. (1991). Effects of maternal employment and child-care arrangements on pre-schoolers' cognitive and behavioural outcomes. *Developmental Psychology, 27,* 932–45.

Beck, A.T. (1976). *Cognitive Therapy and the Emotional Disorders.* New York: Penguin Books.

Belsky, J. and Rovine, M. (1987). Temperament and attachment security in the strange situation: a rapprochement. *Child Development, 58,* 787–95.

Bickman, L. (1974). Clothes make the person. *Psychology Today, 8* (4), 48–51.

Bouchard, T. and McGue, M. (1981). Familial studies of intelligence: a review. *Science, 212,* 1055–59.

Bowlby, J. (1944). Forty-four juvenile thieves: their characters and home lives. *International Journal of Psychoanalysis, 25,* 107–27.

Bowlby, J. (1951). *Maternal Care and Mental Health.* Geneva: World Health Organisation.

Bowlby, J. (1953). *Child Care and the Growth of Love.* Harmondsworth: Penguin Books.

Bowlby, J. (1969). *Attachment and Loss: Vol. 1, Attachment.* London: Hogarth.

BPS (2001). *Code of Ethics and Conduct.* Leicester: British Psychological Society.

Brady, J.V. (1958). Ulcers in executive monkeys. *Scientific American, 199,* 95–100.

Brewer, M.B. (1979). In group bias in the minimal intergroup situation: a cognitive motivational analysis. *Psychological Bulletin, 86*, 307–324.

Brown, G.W. and Harris, T.O. (1978). *Social Origins of Depression: a Study of Psychiatric Disorder in Women*. London: Tavistock Publications.

Brown, R. and McNeill, D. (1966). The 'tip-of-the-tongue' phenomenon. *Journal of Verbal Learning and Verbal Behavior, 5*, 325–37.

Browning, C. (1992). *Ordinary Men: Reserve Police Battalion 101 and the Final Solution in Poland*. New York: HarperCollins.

Bruch, H. (1979). *The Golden Cage*. New York: Vintage Books.

Buehler, R., Griffin, D. and Ross, M. (1994). Exploring the 'planning fallacy': why people underestimate their task completion times. *Journal of Personality and Social Psychology, 67*, 366–81.

Burger, J.M. (1992). *Desire for Control: Personality, Social and Clinical Perspectives*. New York: Plenum.

Buss, D. (1989). Sex differences in human mate preferences. *Behavioural and Brain Sciences, 12*, 1–49.

Campbell, A.J., Cumming, S.R. and Hughes, I. (2006). Internet use by the socially fearful: addiction or therapy? *CyberPsychology and Behaviour, 9* (1), 69–81.

Cannon, W.B. (1927). The James-Lange theory of emotions: a critical examination and an alternative theory. *American Journal of Psychology, 39*, 106–24.

Cattell, R.B. (1971). *Abilities: Their Structure, Growth, and Action*. New York: Houghton Mifflin.

Clarke-Stewart, K.A. (1989). Infant day care: maligned or malignant? *American Psychologist, 44*, 266–73.

Cohen, C.E. (1981). Person categories and social perception: testing some boundaries of the processing effects of prior knowledge. *Journal of Personality and Social Psychology, 40*, 441–52.

Cohen, F., Tyrrell, D.A.J. and Smith, A.P. (1991). Psychological stress and susceptibility to the common cold. *New England Journal of Medicine, 325*, 606–12.

Colman, A.M. (1987). *Facts, Fallacies and Frauds in Psychology*. London: Routledge.

Colten, M.E. and Gore, S. (1991). *Adolescent Stress: Causes and Consequences*. Piscataway, New Jersey: Transaction Publishing.

Cook, M. (1978). *Perceiving Others*. London: Routledge.

Craik, F.I.M. and Tulving, E. (1975). Depth of processing and the retention of words in episodic memory. *Journal of Experimental Psychology: General, 104*, 268–94.

Curtiss, S. (1977). *Genie: A Psycholinguistic Study of a Modern-day 'Wild Child'*. London: Academic Press.

Cutrona, C., Russell, D. and Rose, J. (1986). Social support and adaptation to stress in the elderly. *Psychology and Aging, 1* (1), 47–54.

Deutsch, M. and Gerrard, H.B. (1955). A study of normative and informational influence upon individual judgement. *Journal of Abnormal and Social Psychology, 51*, 629–36.

Dollard, J. and Miller, N.E. (1950). *Personality and Psychotherapy*. New York: McGraw-Hill.

Duncan, J., Seitz, R.J., Kolodny, J., Bor, D., Herzog, H., Ahmed, A., Newell, F.N. and Emslie, H. (2000). A neural basis for general intelligence. *Science, 289*, 457–59.

Durkin, K. (1995). *Developmental Social Psychology: from Infancy to Old Age*. Malden: Wiley-Blackwell.

Eagly, A.H. (1987). *Sex Differences in Social Behaviour: A Social-Role Interpretation*. Hillsdale, New Jersey: Lawrence Erlbaum.

Elliot, J. (1977). The power and pathology of prejudice. In P.G. Zimbardo and F.L. Ruch (eds), *Psychology and Life* (9th ed.). Glenview, IL: Scott, Foresman.

Elliott, R. and Freire, B. (2008). Person-centred/experiential therapies are highly effective: summary of the 2008 meta-analysis. *British Association for the Person-Centred Approach*; http://www.bapca.co.uk [accessed September 2010].

Eysenck, M.W. (1986). Working memory. In G. Cohen, M.W. Eysenck and M.A. Le Voi (eds), *Memory: A Cognitive Approach*. Milton Keynes: Open University Press.

Fiske, S.T. and Taylor, S.E. (1991). *Social Cognition*. New York: McGraw-Hill.

Fleshner, M. (2000). Exercise and neuroendocrine regulation of antibody production: protective effect of physical activity on stress-induced suppression of the specific antibody response. *International Journal of Sports Medicine, 21*, 14–15.

Flynn, J.R. (1984). The mean IQ of Americans: massive gains 1932 to 1978. *Psychological Bulletin, 95* (1), 29–51.

References

Forward, S. (1997). *Emotional Blackmail: When the People in Your Life Use Fear, Obligation and Guilt to Manipulate You*. London: Transworld.

Frankenhauser, M., Dunne, E. and Lundberg, U. (1976). Sex-differences in sympathetic-adrenal medullary reactions induced by different stressors. *Psychopharmacology, 47,* 1–5.

Freedman, J.L. and Fraser, S.C. (1966). Compliance without pressure: the foot-in-the-door technique. *Journal of Personality and Social Psychology, 4,* 195–202.

Freud, S. (1909). Analysis of a phobia in a five year old boy. In *The Pelican Freud Library* (1977), Vol. 8, Case Histories 1, 169–308.

Freud, S. (1910). The origin and development of psychoanalysis. (Translated by H. W. Chase.) *American Journal of Psychology, 21,* 181–218.

Friedman, M. and Rosenman, R.H. (1974). *Type A Behaviour and Your Heart*. New York: Harper Row.

Gamson, W.B., Fireman, B. and Rytina, S. (1982). *Encounters with Unjust Authority*. Hounwood, IL: Dorsey Press.

Gardner, H. (1983). *Frames of Mind: The Theory of Multiple Intelligences*. New York: Basic Books.

Gathercole, S.E. and Baddeley, A.D. (1990). Phonological memory deficits in language disordered children: is there a causal connection? *Journal of Memory and Language, 29* (3), 336–60.

Gavin, J., Duffield, J., Brosnan, M., Joiner, R., Maras, P. and Scott, A. (2007). Drawing the net: internet identification, internet use, and the image of internet users. *CyberPsychology and Behavior, 10* (3), 478–81.

Geiselman, R., Fisher, R., Mackinnon, D. and Holland, H.L. (1985). Enhancement of eyewitness testimony with the cognitive interview. *American Journal of Psychology, 99,* 385–401.

Gladwell, M. (2005). *Blink: The power of thinking without thinking*. London: Penguin Books.

Glanzer, M. and Cunitz, A.R. (1966). Two storage mechanisms in free recall. *Journal of Verbal Learning and Verbal Behavior, 5,* 351–60.

Glass, D.C., Singer, J.E. and Friedman, L.N. (1969). Psychic cost of adaptation to an environmental stressor. *Journal of Personality and Social Psychology, 12,* 200–10.

Goodwin, R. (1999). *Personal Relationships Across Cultures*. London: Routledge.

Gould, S.J. (1982). A nation of morons. *New Scientist, 6,* 349–52.

Greer, A., Morris, T. and Pettingdale, K.W. (1979). Psychological response to breast cancer: effect on outcome. *The Lancet, 13,* 785–87.

Harlow, H.F. (1959). Love in infant monkeys. *Scientific American, 200* (6), 688–74.

Harris, A. (1992). Dialogues as transitional space. In N. Sckolnick (ed.), *Relational Perspectives in Psychoanalysis*. Hillsdale, New Jersey: Analytic Press.

Hart, B. and Risley, T. (1995). *Meaningful Differences in Everyday Parenting and Intellectual Development in Young American Children*. Baltimore: Brookes.

Hazan, C. and Shaver, P.R. (1987). Romantic love conceptualised as an attachment process. *Journal of Personality and Social Psychology, 52,* 511–24.

Hill, R. (1970). *Family Development in Three Generations*. Cambridge, MA: Schenkman.

Hodges, J. and Tizard, B. (1989). Social and family relationships of ex-institutionalised adolescents. *Journal of Child Psychology and Psychiatry, 30,* 77–97.

Hofling, C.K., Brotzman, E., Dalrymple, S., Graves, N. and Pierce, C.M. (1966). An experimental study in nurse-physician relationships. *Journal of Nervous and Mental Disease, 143,* 171–80.

Holt-Lunstad, J., Smith, T.B. and Layton, J.B. (2010). Social relationships and mortality risk: a meta-analytic review. *PLoS Med 7* (7): e1000316. doi:10.1371/journal.pmed.1000316

Horn, J.M. (1983). The Texas Adoption Project: adopted children and their intellectual resemblance to biological and adoptive parents. *Child Development, 54,* 266–75.

Hornsey, M.J., Spears, R., Cremers, I. and Hogg, M.A. (2003). Relations between high and low power groups: the importance of legitimacy. *Personality and Social Psychology Bulletin, 29,* 216–27.

Ivancevich, J.M. and Matteson, M.T. (1980). *Stress and Work: A Managerial Perspective*. Glenview, IL: Foresman.

Jenness, A. (1932). The role of discussion in changing opinion regarding matter of fact. *Journal of Abnormal and Social Psychology, 27,* 279–96.

Jennings, H.H. (1950). *Leadership and Isolation*. New York: Longman.

Johansson, G., Aronsson, G. and Linstrom, B.O. (1978). Social psychological and neuroendocrine stress reactions in highly mechanized work. *Ergonomics, 21,* 583–99.

Johnson, J.H. and Sarason, I.G. (1978). Life stress, depression and anxiety: internal/external control as a moderator variable. *Journal of Psychosomatic Research, 22*, 205–08.

Katz, D. and Braly, K.W. (1933). Racial stereotypes of 100 college students. *Journal of Abnormal and Social Psychology, 288*, 280–90.

Kelman, H. (1958). Compliance, internalisation and identification: three processes of attitude change. *Journal of Conflict Resolution, 2*, 51–60.

Kempermann, G., Kuhn, H.G. and Gage, F.H. (1997). More hippocampal neurons in adult mice living in an enriched environment. *Nature, 386*, 493–95.

Kiecolt-Glaser, J.K., Garner, W., Speicher, C.E., Penn, G.M., Holliday, J. and Glaser, R. (1984). Psychosocial modifiers of immunocompetence in medical students. *Psychosomatic Medicine, 46*, 7–14.

Kim, H.K. and McKenry, P.C. (1998). Social networks and support: a comparison of African Americans, Asian Americans, Caucasians and Hispanics. *Journal of Comparative and Family Studies, 29*, 313–36.

Klein, M. (1957). *Envy and Gratitude*. London: Tavistock.

Kohlberg, L. (1969). *Stages in the Development of Moral Thought and Action*. New York: Holt.

Koluchová, J. (1991). Severely deprived twins after 22 years observation. *Studia Psychologica, 33*, 23–28.

Kulik, J.A. and Kulik, C.C. (1992). Meta-analytic findings on grouping programs. *Gifted Children Quarterly, 36*, 73–77.

Laar, C.V., Levin, S., Sinclair, S. and Sidanius, J. (2005). The effect of university roommate contact on ethnic attitudes and behavior. *Journal of Experimental and Social Psychology, 41*, 329–45.

Lamb, M.E. (1981). The development of father–infant relationships. In M.E. Lamb (ed.), *The Role of the Father in Child Development*. New York: Wiley.

LaPiere, R.T. (1934). Attitudes vs actions. *Social Forces, 13*, 230–37.

Lazarus, R.S. and Folkman, S. (1984). *Stress, Appraisal and Coping*. New York: Springer.

Lemyre, L. and Smith, P.M. (1985). Intergroup discrimination and self-esteem in the minimal group paradigm. *Journal of Psychology, 49*, 660–670.

Loftus, E.F. and Palmer, J.C. (1974). Reconstruction of automobile destruction: an example of the interaction between language and memory. *Journal of Verbal Learning and Verbal Behavior, 13*, 585–89.

Maccoby, E.E. (1980). *Social Development – Psychological Growth and the Parent–Child Relationship*. New York: Harcourt Brace Jovanovich.

McGuffin, P., Katz, R., Rutherford, J. and Watkins, S. (1996). The heritability of DSM-IV unipolar depression: a hospital based twin register study. *Archives of General Psychiatry, 53*, 129–36.

Maslow, A. (1943). A theory of human motivation. *Psychological Review, 50*, 370–96.

Meichenbaum, D. (1977). *Cognitive-Behaviour Modification: An Integrative Approach*. New York: Plenum Press.

Milgram, S. (1963). Behavioural study of obedience. *Journal of Abnormal and Social Psychology, 67*, 371–78.

Milgram, S. (1974). *Obedience to Authority*. New York: Harper and Row.

Miller, G.A. (1956). The magical number seven, plus or minus two: some limits on our capacity for processing information. *Psychological Review, 63* (2), 343–55.

Miller, K. (2005). *Communication Theories*. New York: McGraw Hill.

Morris, J.N., Heady, J.A., Raffle, P.A.B., Roberts, C.G. and Parks, J.W. (1953). Coronary heart-disease and physical activity of work. *Lancet, 2*, 1053; 1111.

Morris, P.E., Tweedy, M. and Gruneberg, M.M. (1985). Interest, knowledge, and the memorising of soccer scores. *British Journal of Psychology, 76*, 415–25.

Moscovici, S. (1981). On social representations. In J.P. Forgas (ed.), *Social Cognition: Perspectives in Everyday Understanding*. London: Academic Press.

Mumford, D.B., Whitehouse, A.M. and Plattes, M. (1991). Sociocultural correlates of eating disorders among Asian schoolgirls in Bradford. *British Journal of Psychiatry, 158*, 222–28.

Murstein, B.I. (1972). Physical attractiveness and marital choice. *Journal of Personality and Social Psychology, 22* (1), 8–12.

Neisser, U., Boodoo, G., Bouchard, T.J., Boykin, A.W., Brody, N., Ceci, S.J., Halpern, D.F., Loehlin, J.C., Perloff, R., Sternberg, R.J. and Urbina, S. (1996). Intelligence: knowns and unknowns. *American Psychologist, 51*, 77–101.

Ng, C., Schweitzer, I., Alexopolous, P., Celi, E., Wong, L., Tuckwell, V., Sergejew, A. and Tiller, J. (2000). Efficacy and cognitive effects of right unilateral electro-convulsive therapy. *Journal of ECT, 16*, 370–79.

References

Nuckolls, K.B., Cassel, J. and Kaplan, B.H. (1972). Psychological assets, life crisis and the prognosis of pregnancy. *American Journal of Epidemiology, 95*, 431–41.

Pavlov, I.P. (1927). *Conditioned Reflexes*. Oxford: Oxford University Press.

Perrin, S. and Spencer, C. (1980). The Asch effect: a child of its time. *Bulletin of the British Psychological Society, 33*, 405–06.

Peterson, L.R. and Peterson, M.J. (1959). Short-term retention of individual verbal items. *Journal of Experimental Psychology, 58*, 193–98.

Piliavin, I.M., Rodin, J. and Piliavin, J.A. (1969). Good Samaritanism: an underground phenomenon? *Journal of Personality and Social Psychology, 13*, 289–99.

Rahe, R.H., Mahan, J. and Arthur, R. (1970). Predictions of near-future health-change from subjects' preceding life changes. *Journal of Psychosomatic Research, 14*, 401–06.

Rank, S.G. and Jacobson, C.K. (1977). Hospital nurses' compliance with medication overdose orders: a failure to replicate. *Journal of Health and Social Behavior, 18*, 188–93.

Ridley, M. (2003). *Nature Via Nurture*. London: Fourth Estate Publishing.

Robertson, J. and Robertson, J. (1967–73). Film Series, *Young Children in Brief Separation, No. 3* (1969). John, 17 months, 9 days in a residential nursery. London: Tavistock.

Robinson, K. (2001). *Out of our Minds: Learning to be Creative*. Chichester, West Sussex: Capstone Publishing.

Rogers, C. (1951). *Client-centred Therapy: Its Current Practices, Implications and Theory*. Boston: Houghton-Mifflin.

Rosenhan, D.L. (1973). On being sane in insane places. *Science, 179*, 250–58.

Rosenthal, R. and Jacobson, L. (1968). *Pygmalion in the Classroom: Teacher Expectation and Pupils' Intellectual Development*. New York: Holt, Rinehart & Winston.

Rotter, J.B. (1966). Generalised expectancies for internal versus external control of reinforcement. *Psychological Monographs, 80*, 1–28.

Rubin, M. and Hewstone, M. (1998). Social identity theory's self-esteem hypothesis: a review and some suggestions for clarification. *Personality and Social Psychology Review, 2* (1), 40–62.

Rubin, Z. (1973). *Liking and Loving: An Invitation to Social Psychology*. New York: Holt, Rinehart & Winston.

Rutter, M. (1976). Parent–child separation: psychological effects on the child. In A.M. Clarke and A.D.B. Clark (eds), *Early Experience: Myth and Evidence*. London: Open Books.

Rutter, M. (1981). *Maternal Deprivation Reassessed* (2nd ed.). Harmondsworth: Penguin.

Rutter, M. and the ERA study team (1998). Developmental catch-up, and deficit, following adoption after severe global early privation. *Journal of Child Psychiatry, 39* (4), 465–76.

Saegert, S., Swap, W. and Zajonc, R.B. (1973). Exposure, contact and interpersonal attraction. *Journal of Personality and Social Psychology, 25*, 234–42.

Scarr, S. (1998). American child care today. *American Psychologist, 53* (2), 95–108.

Schachter, S. and Singer, J.E. (1962). Cognitive, social and physiological determinants of emotional state. *Psychological Review, 69*, 379–99.

Schaffer, H.R. (1996). *Social Development*. Oxford: Blackwell.

Schaffer, H.R. and Emerson, P.E. (1964). The development of social attachments in infancy. *Monographs of the Society for Research in Child Development, 29* (3), serial no. 94.

Schweickert, R. and Boruff, B. (1986). Short-term memory capacity: magic number or magic spell? *Journal of Experimental Psychology: Learning, Memory and Cognition, 12*, 419–45.

Scoville, W.B. and Milner, B. (1957). Loss of recent memory after bilateral hippocampal lesions. *Journal of Neurology, Neurosurgery and Psychiatry, 20*, 11–21.

Selye, H. (1936). A syndrome produced by diverse nocuous agents. *Nature, 138*, 32.

Selye, H. (1956). *The Stress of Life*. New York: McGraw-Hill.

Shapiro, D.A., Barkham, M., Rees, A., Hardy, G.E., Reynolds, S. and Startup, M. (1994). Effects of treatment duration and severity of depression on the effectiveness of cognitive–behavioral and psychodynamic–interpersonal psychotherapy. *Journal of Consulting and Clinical Psychology, 62* (3), 522–34.

Sheridan, C.L. and King, R.G. (1972). Obedience to authority with an authentic victim. *Proceedings of the 80th Annual Convention, American Psychological Association, 7* (1), 165–66.

Sherif, M. (1935). A study of some factors in perception. *Archives of Psychology, 27* (187), 1–60.

Sherif, M., Harvey, O.J., White, B.J., Hood, W.R. and Sherif, C.W. (1954). *Experimental Study of Positive and Negative Intergroup Attitudes between Experimentally Produced Groups*. Oklahoma: University of Oklahoma Press.

Skeels, H.M. and Dye, H.B. (1939). A study of the effects of differential stimulation on mentally retarded children. *Proceedings and Addresses, American Association for Mental Defectiveness, 44*, 114–15.

Smith, C.R. (1991). Learning Disabilities: *The Interaction of Learner, Task and Setting*. Boston, MA: Allyn and Bacon.

Smith, P. and Bond, M.H. (1993). *Social Psychology Across Cultures: Analysis and Perspectives*. New York: Harvester Wheatsheaf.

Spearman, C. (1904). 'General intelligence' objectively determined and measured. *American Journal of Psychology, 15*, 201–93.

Sperling, G. (1960). The information available in brief visual presentations. *Psychological Monographs, 74* (11), 1–29.

Spitz, R.A. and Wolf, K.M. (1946). Anaclitic depression. *Psychoanalytic Study of the Child, 2*, 313–42.

Sternberg, R. (1988). *The Triarchic Mind: A New Theory of Intelligence*. New York: Viking Press.

Sternberg, R.J. and Grigorenko, E.L. (2004). Successful intelligence in the classroom. *Theory Into Practice, 43*, 274–80.

Tache, J., Selye, H. and Day, S. (1979*). Cancer, Stress and Death*. New York: Plenum Press.

Tajfel, H. (1970). Experiments in intergroup discrimination. *Scientific American, 223*, 96–105.

Tajfel, H. and Turner, J.C. (1979). An integrative theory of intergroup conflict. In W.G. Austin and S. Worchel (eds), *The Social Psychology of Intergroup Relations*. Monterey, CA: Brooks, Cole.

Taylor, S.E., Klein, L.C., Lewis, B.P., Gruenewald, T.L., Gurung, R.A.R. and Updegraff, J.A. (2000). Biobehavioural responses to stress in females: Tend-and-befriend, not fight-or-flight. *Psychological Review, 107* (3), 411–29.

Thibaut, J.W. and Kelley, H.H. (1959). *The Social Psychology of Groups*. New York: Wiley.

Thigpen, C. and Cleckley, H. (1954). A case of multiple personality. *Journal of Abnormal and Social Psychology, 49*, 135–51.

Thurstone, L.L. and Thurstone, T.G. (1941). Factorial studies of intelligence. *Psychometric Monographs, 2*, 9.

Tosun, L. and Lajunen, T. (2010). Does Internet use reflect your personality? Relationship between Eysenck's personality dimensions and Internet use. *Computers in Human Behavior, 26* (2), 162–67.

Van Ijzendoorn, M.H. and Kroonenberg, P.M. (1988). Cross-cultural patterns of attachment: a meta-analysis of the strange situation. *Child Development, 59*, 147–56.

Walker, M.P., Brakefield, T., Hobson, J.A. and Stickgold, R. (2003). Dissociable stages of human memory consolidation and reconsolidation. *Nature, 425*, 616–20.

Walster, E.H., Aronson, E., Abrahams, D. and Rottman, L. (1966). Importance of physical attractiveness in dating behaviour. *Journal of Personality and Social Psychology, 4*, 325–42.

Walster, E.H., Walster, G.W. and Berscheid, E. (1978). *Equity Theory and Research*. Boston: Allyn & Bacon.

Watson, J. and Rayner, R. (1920). Conditioned emotional responses. *Journal of Experimental Psychology, 63*, 575–82.

Waugh, N.C. and Norman, D.A. (1965). Primary memory. *Psychological Review, 72*, 89–104.

Wechsler, D. (1940). Non-intellective factors in general intelligence. *Psychological Bulletin, 37*, 444–45.

Wilson, G.T. (1996). Treatment of bulimia nervosa: When CBT Fails. *Behavior Research and Therapy, 34 (3)*, 197–112.

Youssef, H.A. and Youssef, F.A. (1999). Time to abandon electroconvulsion as a treatment in modern psychiatry. *Advances in Therapy, 16* (1), 29–38.

Yuille, J.C. and Cutshall, J.L. (1986). A case study of eyewitness testimony of a crime. *Journal of Applied Psychology, 71*, 291–301.

Zimbardo, P.G., Banks, P.G., Haney, C. and Jaffe, D. (1973). Pirandellian prison: the mind is a formidable jailor. *New York Times Magazine*, 8 April, 38–60.

Acknowledgments

Leckie and Leckie is grateful to the following copyright holders for permission to use their material:

- Graph (p. 5): Schaffer, H.R. and Emerson, P.E. (1964). The development of social attachments in infancy. *Monographs of the Society for Research in Child Development, 29 (3)*, serial no. 94. Wiley Blackwell.
- Table (p. 9):Van Ijzendoorn, M.H. and Kroonenberg, P.M. (1988). Cross-cultural patterns of attachment: a meta-analysis of the strange situation. *Child Development, 59*, 147–56. Wiley Blackwell.
- Graph (p. 64): Asch, S.E. (1955). Opinions and social pressure. *Scientific American*, 193, 31–35. *Scientific American*, a division of Nature America, Inc.

We would like to thank the following for permission to reproduce photographs. Page numbers are in brackets and are followed, where necessary, by t (top), b (bottom), m (middle), l (left) or r (right).

- ADAGP, Paris and DACS: 58
- Barry Austin: 37
- BananaStock: 4m, 30m
- Michael Blann: 74
- Brand X Pictures: 63b
- Comstock Images: 4b, 23, 94t
- Digital Vision: 30t
- George Doyle: 86
- iStockphoto: 7b, 10, 17, 19, 24t, 28, 32, 36, 42, 68, 83l, 83r, 96
- Jupiterimages: 7t, 14, 44, 53, 63t, 67t, 76t, 76b
- Alexandra Milgram: 66
- Barbara Penoyar: 94b
- Photodisc: 55, 67b
- Photos.com: 56
- Pixland: 30b
- Rayes: 4t, 72
- Science Photo Library: cover, 6
- Stockbyte: 9
- Tate Images: 58
- Karl Weatherly: 80

Index